GW00659965

Human Being Human

Human Being Human explores the classical question 'What is a human being?'

In examining our human *being*, Christopher Hauke challenges the notion of human nature, questions the assumed superiority of human consciousness and rational thinking and pays close attention to the contradiction of living simultaneously as an autonomous individual and a member of the collective community. The main chapters include:

- Who's in charge here? Knowledge, power and human being
- That thinking feeling
- Is modern consciousness different? Modern consciousness and the quest for spirituality
- Endings, the unconscious and time
- Orpheus, Dionysus and popular culture

The book is also structured around brief panel essays with a distinctly personal tone, such as: The rise of revulsion: spitting and The Stones, What is the double when the original is gone? And 'I lived with the speaking clock'. All these themes are amplified by examples drawn from psychotherapy, film, literature and popular culture, and illustrated with many evocative photographs and film stills.

Human Being Human provides an original perspective on what it is to be a human being, the value of popular culture, the relationship between the individual and the collective and our assumptions about truth, reality and power. Written in a highly accessible style, this book is both intellectually and emotionally satisfying and will fascinate anyone interested in contemporary psychology, cultural studies, film and media, social history and psychotherapy.

Christopher Hauke is a Jungian analyst in private practice, a lecturer at Goldsmiths College, University of London and a film-maker. He is author of *Jung and the Postmodern: The Interpretation of Realities*, and co-editor of *Jung and Film: Post-Jungian Takes on the Moving Image* and *Contemporary Jungian Analysis*.

Contact the author at mail@humanbeinghuman.net

Human Being Human

Culture and the Soul

Christopher Hauke

Routledge
Taylor & Francis Group

LONDON AND NEW YORK

First published 2005 by Routledge
27 Church Road, Hove, East Sussex, BN3 2FA

Simultaneously published in the US and Canada
by Routledge
270 Madison Avenue, New York. NY 10016

Routledge is an imprint of the Taylor & Francis Group

© 2005 Christopher Hauke

Typeset in Palatino by
Keystroke, Jacaranda Lodge, Wolverhampton
Printed and bound in Great Britain by
TJ International Ltd, Padstow, Cornwall
Paperback cover design by Lisa Dynan

This publication has been produced with paper manufactured
to strict environmental standards and with pulp derived from
sustainable forests.

British Library Cataloguing in Publication Data
A catalogue record for this book is available from the British Library

Library of Congress Cataloging in Publication Data
Hauke, Christopher, 1953–
    Human being human : culture and the soul/Christopher Hauke.
        p. cm.
    Includes bibliographical references (p.) and index.
    ISBN 1–58391–714–4 (hbk) — ISBN 1–58391–715–2 (pbk)
    1. Psychoanalysis and culture. 2. Consciousness.
    3. Jungian psychology. I. Title.
    BF175.4.C84H37 2005
    150.19'54—dc22

                                                        2005012596

ISBN 1–58391–714–4 (hbk)
ISBN 1–58391–715–2 (pbk)

For my parents
Adolph and Sylvia.

With love and thanks for making me a human; I guess the
rest is up to me . . .

CONTENTS

LIST OF FILMS

21 Grams (Gonzalez-Inarritu, Alejandro, 2003)
Alive (Marshall, Frank, 1993)
American Beauty (Mendes, Sam, 1999)
Apocalypse Now (Coppola, Francis Ford, 1979)
Birth (Glazer, Jonathan, 2004)
Blackboard Jungle (Brooks, Richard, 1955)
Blade Runner (Scott, Ridley, 1982)
The Bourne Identity (Liman, Doug, 2002)
Cold Mountain (Minghella, Anthony, 2003)
Dr Doolitle (Thomas, Betty, 1998)
Easy Rider (Hopper, Dennis 1969)
Feeding the Baby (Lumiere Brothers, 1896)
Gladiator (Scott, Ridley, 2000)
The Graduate (Nichols, Mike, 1967)
Groundhog Day (Ramis, Harold, 1993)
The Guns of Navarone (Thompson, J. Lee, 1961)
A Hard Day's Night (Lester, Dick, 1964)
Kagemusha: The Shadow Warrior (Kurosawa, Akira, 1980)
Me, Myself and Irene (Farrelly, Bobby and Peter, 2000)
Midnight Cowboy (Schlesinger, John, 1969)
The Navigator: A Medieval Odyssey (Ward, Vincent, 1988)
One Hour Photo (Romanek, Mark, 2002)
Orphee (Cocteau, Jean, 1949)
The Piano (Campion, Jane, 1993)
Pleasantville (Ross, Gary, 1998)
Psycho (Hitchcock, Alfred, 1960)

LIST OF ILLUSTRATIONS

PERMISSIONS

The following permissions to quote from other works have been gratefully received. Extract from the novel *Pilgrim* by Timothy Findley (Faber and Faber Ltd., UK and Harper*Flamingo* Canada, 1999). Copyright 1999 Pebble Productions Inc. With permission of Pebble Productions Inc. Quotations from Jung, C. G.; *The Collected Works of C.G. Jung*. Translator, Hull, R. F. C., 1977 Princeton University Press, USA and Routledge Publishers, UK. An earlier version of the chapter 'Racism, incest and the split mind of modernity: everyone is now a stranger among strangers' was published by Rebus Press in 1996 in the volume *Teaching Transference* edited by Martin Stanton and David Reason. The chapter 'Orpheus, Dionysus and popular culture: Jean Cocteau's *Orphee* – then and now' has been adapted from the version originally published in *Spring. A Journal of Archetype and Culture*. Issue 71, "Orpheus", Fall, 2004, pp. 127-142.

Apart from the film stills sourced from the Kobal Collection, all photographs, including those on the cover, are by C. C. Hauke, except "Mother and Child" by A.C. Hauke and are used by permission with all rights reserved.

Every effort has been made to trace copyright holders and obtain permission for quoted material. Any omissions brought to our attention will be remedied in future editions.

FOREWORD
by Luke Hockley

There I was in my study working on an academic paper when the phone rang. I didn't know it would be an analyst on the other end of the line let alone Chris Hauke – at that point I didn't even know who he was. I'd better explain.

As a film arts graduate and academic film theorist the inner mysteries of the consulting room and couch were for me just the stuff of movies. Perhaps this is not that surprising as it must be clear to anyone that clinical psychoanalysis and film-making are miles apart. Yet that phone call was to bring together for me those two quite separate worlds and to lead to some of the best collaborative experiences I've ever had. Chris asked me to contribute to *Jung and Film* a book which has subsequently become a landmark in Jungian film criticism. Since then Chris and I have travelled and lectured together in the UK, Europe and most recently in the USA.

Of course, over the last five years I've come to realise that being a Jungian analyst is only one aspect of who Chris Hauke is and it is the very richness and diversity of his background that makes him such a fascinating and rewarding person to know. Trained as an actor, also a musician, then as an analyst, Chris has recently discovered his passion and gift for making films. Slowly I've come to see that film-making and therapy are not such different activities. They both involve listening, watching and editing (rearranging events to make sense of someone's story); both are profoundly creative and transformatory acts. It is the ability to see the potential in a life, in a story, in a film that shines through this book as they reflect and refract each other.

It is through relationships with people like Chris, and via his films, that we find the world transformed into a place where toughness can become a tender, strong and compassionate. You'll find this quality throughout *Human Being Human*. It's deeply rooted in a concern with letting us explore in words, images and actions who we are, not just what life has turned us into.

In my experience it's rare to find someone with a genuine ability to think in new, insightful and thoughtful ways. It is also unusual to find someone who has a real capacity to care; to find them in one person is remarkable. Yet it's not. What this book has helped me to realise is that far from being unusual this is actually what being human is all about. Like the best movies, it was a pleasure to be caught out by a wonderful surprise ending.

ACKNOWLEDGEMENTS

Over the years I have talked with a lot of people – great conversations over beers in Norman's in Greek Street or cocktails at No.1 Aldwych in London, or breakfast in the NoHo Star on Spring Street, or watching baseball in some Greenwich Village bar, or on a boat on Washington Lake, outside a café in some little Italian town, eating steaks in the French Quarter or near Union Square (on both coasts), and even some times when there was no eating or drinking involved at all. We were probably walking around at the time. Or on a train. Or driving. Or half-watching a movie or TV or listening to the Yardbirds or Boz Scaggs or Ray Charles. Anyway, you all know who you are and if you're not in this list it's not because we're not friends but most likely the fact that I am checking across an address book that has been imperfectly copied from at least three predecessors. Not to mention the cell-phone list (both SIM and Phone List, just to make it harder) and then the email addresses. (How are you meant to copy those when the OS keeps changing and your first computer was a 386?)

I digress. All these great conversations and meetings have worked their way into these pages. Everyone I am about to mention has made a lovely, stimulating, fresh and encouraging contribution to everything I offer in this book. They have also added to the richness of my creative life in the film projects that have accompanied my writing over the last two years, and continue with their support as we embark on further writing and filming adventures.

In the zone of psychotherapy and Jungian studies my heart

goes to thank Andrew Samuels – a solid gold supporter from day one – and Michael Vannoy Adams, who have backed up, argued with and developed my ideas more than they realise. I also want to thank the Boyz from the 'hood, Luke Hockley and Anshu Srivastava for just the same reasons.

For their invitations and for their hospitality, in addition to their conversation and support, I wish to thank Beverley and Phillip Zabriskie and Una Chauduri of New York, Nancy and Glen Cater of Spring Publications, New Orleans, John Beebe of San Francisco, Lee Leatherwood in Austin, and in Seattle, Michael and Diane Horne, Sharon Green, Ladson Hinton and Dan Barr.

I am also grateful to the filmmakers who have responded to my interest and shared their views along the way especially Nick Morris and Jonathan Glazer of Academy, Paul Morrison and John White of APT, Eva Ziemsen, Isabel Rocamora, Alwyn Gosford, and Paul Thompson of NYU. As well as my collaborative friends and critics Rob Thom and Serge Soric, and especially Ray Bowler who, frankly, has more to say than me. Polona Curk, Imogen Burch and Claire Lipscomb have been the greatest help in the preparation of the book for publication. Tessa Adams, Jan Campbell, Anastasios Gaitanidis, Janet Kaylo, Susan Rowland, Martin Stanton, Max Velmans, Paul Wadey, Mary Wilson, Bob Withers and others at Goldsmiths and south of the river have all added more than they realise.

Once again I thank F. David Peat for his friendship and being sixteen books ahead of me! For memorable conversations and their encouragement, I also thank May Arnaot, Susan Berger, Anne Casement, Don Fredericksen, Alan Jones, Barbara Black Koltuv, Paul Kugler, Justin Lorentzen, Dale Mathers, Anne and Alan McFarlane, Tony Slater, Peter Tatham, David and Dee Williams, and Angelika Yiassemides. Finally thanks to Steven Hughes, Philip Dodd, Anthony Denslow and Raj Persaud at the BBC. And to paraphrase D.W. Winnicott, may I thank all my clients for paying me to learn from them. Once again I thank Sue, Jessica, Joseph, Matt and Ben for . . . well, you know what for.

London, August 2005

1

Introduction: Human Being or 'Human Nature'

Great philosophers and popular storytellers alike have all pondered the question of 'What makes us human?' While Immanuel Kant reckoned 'The greatest human quest is to know what one must *do* in order to be a human being', Descartes only had to *think* to know he existed as a human being. Similar to Plato years before, Descartes concluded that *consciousness* was the quality that distinguished humans from all other forms of being. Where they differed, however, was that Plato realised we only had a dim, shadowy version of this human attribute, a 1.1 issue of the software if you like.

Modern philosopher John Gray asserts, 'Being a person is not the essence of humanity, only – as the word's history suggests – one of its masks'. The idea of a person defined by one who 'authors her own life through her choices' is a relatively modern one, he claims.[1] In Ridley Scott's movie *Blade Runner* (1982), Deckard, played by Harrison Ford, is glad to hunt down and rid his world of replicant humans – androids with some ethical screws loose. But one day he encounters a higher-grade replicant, Rachael, who he judges to be human enough to take as his lover. In Deckard's case what makes a being human is the degree to which he can feel attached to her and care for her. In this story, the essence of being human involves empathy. Indeed, one of the 'tests' to detect a 'real' human being in this world of replicants created as 'more human than human' is a verbal test for empathic responses. The psychologist Don Williams writes of the film as showing ourselves as having 'completed' the Human Genome Project: 'we approach a transition to a post-human era where "human nature" is not "handed down" but continuously revised, extended, and refined in a process of ongoing creation'.[2]

But this view flies in the face of what many believe when they refer to human nature. For hundreds if not thousands of years, the phrase and concept human nature has indicated something fundamental and basic about human beings. It implies that there are universal qualities, behaviours, and emotional and cognitive attitudes to be found in every human being. It does not imply universal beliefs necessarily, these are allowed to vary, but it does imply ethical values – what a human being should or should not do. I shall go into this business of ethics and standards and the degree to which we allow for differences in Chapter 3. At this point I want to introduce the implications of this idea of 'human nature' that underpins our conception of what it is to be a human being.

First of all, why do we have a problem with what might be the defining characteristics of human nature? Or, even before that, why do we have to state what is human nature? Is it not as self-obvious as stating 'The sky is blue'? Surely any organism born of a human mother is *de facto* a human being. In the same way, any dog born of a female dog is not a human being and is a dog. Even Dolly the Sheep, the first animal to be cloned (after over 400 attempts, I have dis-covered, and leaving behind a trail of genetic failures I am tempted to call Dolly Mixtures) was no less a sheep for all her unusual origins, most would agree. Except in cases where there is extra human intervention (like that of Dolly's), 'biological' nature is such that human beings produce clones spontaneously; when a single fertilized egg splits we call these monozygotic or 'identical' twins. These individuals are not regarded as anything other than human beings with the same 'human nature' as singletons you would think – but there are places and people for whom this is not so clear-cut. The African nomadic group called the Nuer were studied by the anthropologist Evans-Pritchard who reports, 'It seems

2

odd, if not absurd, to a European when he is told that a twin is a bird as though it were an obvious fact, for Nuer are not saying that a twin is *like* a bird but that he *is* a bird . . . no contradiction is involved in the statement . . . to one who presents the idea to himself in the Nuer language and within their system of religious thought . . . They are not saying that a twin has a beak, feathers, and so forth. Nor in their everyday relations as twins do Nuers speak of them as birds or act towards them as though they were birds.'[3]

We could take this in several directions. A Victorian colonial mentality would dismiss the Nuer themselves as less than human simply because they hold such beliefs, and I look at the relationship between colonialism, racism and our conception of human being in Chapter 8. In present times, we may be more inclined to regard the Nuer people's belief about twins pluralistically. We might regard their idea as an example of human differences in the use of concepts (things that are *signified* like the actual physical *thing* that is a bird or a human twin) and differences in the use of words and language (like the word, or *signifier*, 'bird' or the word 'twin'). These days, many anthropologists and philosophers have drawn our attention to the way in which, although language and concepts may vary across different human groups, the fact of *having a language* remains a sure sign of a human being rather than any other sort of being. But the Nuer are adding to the range of definitions of human by calling twins birds. They do not deny twins are human, they simply add that they are birds.

The Nuer's point of view leaves us with a problem of how we distinguish humans because a key western approach has often been to define humans as distinct from animals. Even when humans acknowledge that they are also a type of animal, they like to strengthen the definition of what makes humans distinctive from the rest of the living world by exaggerating their human exclusivity. One tactic has been to claim that all other animals, despite being as different as a shrimp is from an elephant, still have *more in common with each other than any animal has in common with human beings*.

The discussion – or the *need* for any discussion – of what it is to be a human being is forced to take place against thinking that cannot let go of primarily defining humans as differentiated from all other creatures.

Using a typically dualistic paradigm, our thinking makes one particular choice of opposition (the way in which 'human' equals 'not animal'), the most important criteria by which we define what is human. Chapter 2, which follows this introduction, looks more deeply into how we think in opposites. But when it comes to the case of defining what is human, the parameters of this particular opposition vary a great deal. Humans differ in appearance from animals, for instance, but there are also many similarities in morphology when it comes to mammals, and especially primates, so that appearance alone does not suffice.

What about development? All creatures grow from birth to maturity, but human infants are dependent on another's care far longer than is any other creature. Rarely are human beings primarily defined as those organisms who are born insufficiently mature to ensure their survival without massive help from more mature organisms around them. But this is indeed so. A newborn human baby will perish rapidly if there is no attention given to their need for nourishment, body-temperature regulation and protection from harm. Apart from a very important factor that I will introduce in a moment, when viewed from a behavioural point of view, a human baby is born with an extreme inability to get their needs met apart from their powerful cry. This, presumably, innate, mechanism can as easily summon the attention of a predator as a care-giver – an observation that makes us think twice about the evolutionists' reading of behaviours as persisting simply to ensure survival. In brief then, a further definition of our 'essential' human nature – but one that is rarely flagged up as such – is how 'Humans are those unique creatures born utterly unable to look after themselves without help'.[4]

Taking the human/animal duality of similarities and differences further, what is human behaviour as distinct from animal behaviour? Arising from the strategy of oppositional thinking comes the attempt at a definition of human being by analysing what humans do – once again in comparison with other creatures. This is where the irony of defining what it is to be a human being really kicks in. On the one hand, humans are defined by behaviour that is *distinctly human* – that is, behaviour that other creatures do not express. Speech, as has been noted, is the most important and apparently unarguable of these. But on the other hand, humans are also *defined by their similarity* to certain other animals as a way of valuing certain behaviour regarded as 'more human' than is found in other, different creatures. Dogs, many would agree, appear to share a 'human' behaviour in a tendency towards loyalty, but are quite animal-like and non-human in the way they will defecate or copulate in public. On the other hand, wolves, who have an appearance similar to many dogs and a group behaviour that resembles a form of human community, have qualities of predation regarded as ruthless and unlike the behaviour expected of humans. In appearance, ants could hardly appear more different from human beings and yet the leaf-cutting ant reveals behaviour compellingly similar to farming practices, social cooperation and job allocation found in human behaviour but seldom in other creatures.

One behaviour regarded as common to both humans and many animals such as primates, dogs and elephants, is the female adults' nurturance of their young – most commonly undertaken by the birth-mother but seldom by males. The fact that these animals nurture their young in a way that has similarities to human nurturance – feeding, grooming, gazing, protection and attention to distress cries – apparently justifies the view that such behaviour found in humans must therefore be fundamental and qualify as 'human nature'. This brings with it an implication that deviation from (or avoidance of) this behaviour by females is a perversion – that is, 'against (human) nature'. How ironic is that? Here a comparison with the animal is employed in reverse of its usual function: not to clarify human uniqueness and

5

difference but in this case being used to establish the fundamental 'nature' of humans by citing similarities in 'nature' elsewhere in animals. This is the tactic employed by the conservative view that claims for human uniqueness the contradictory facts of both 'free will' and 'natural' instinctive behaviours: what is distinctly human about ourselves (free will) is found in no other creatures as they have behaviour driven by instinct. But at the same time it is being claimed that some human behaviours are distinctly human *because they are instinctively driven*, as we see in animals. The summary goes like this: We are distinctly human because, *unlike* dumb animals, we have the freedom to choose our behaviour. We are also distinctly human because, *similar to* dumb animals, we have behaviours that are naturally human and we only fail to enact these because we are using our free will perversely and making a mistake. It is in our nature to be able to ignore our nature!

This reveals why we need the two-word phrase: human nature. There are clearly two concepts here, but, as the summary shows, from a certain perspective they cannot be regarded separately. Hence I prefer side-stepping the thorny 'nature' aspect of what it is to be human and focus instead on the noun phrase: human being. In my view, this line of thinking can help us move away from biological emphases and towards the question of how we value various human and animal social behaviours. However, such has been the attraction of biological knowledge for those seeking robust scientific confirmations of what it is to be a human being that the discussion frequently slips into using biological concepts to explain or describe behaviour. At best, this approach can be limited and at worst it is downright wrong. For example, creatures such as mice and rats are frequently used for experiments designed to tell us something about neurological processes going on in human brains. In the study of addiction, for instance, rats and mice are subjected to conditions which show they will self-administer pleasurable substances like cocaine to the point at which they neglect food, sex and sleep. It is found that the reward offered

by these substances overrides what are regarded as fundamental survival instincts, thus making the argument for an
essentially biological basis to the addictive power of such
chemicals. The brains of these creatures are examined to add
to our knowledge of how such powerful drug effects are
acting on their neurological systems. Because of the assumption of anatomical and neurological similarity between
human brains and rat brains, the results of these studies are
regarded as informative about the way in which humans
become addicted to substances and as evidence of how they
are compelled to enjoy cocaine and other drugs for biological
reasons.

At the same time, culturally-based studies of human
drug addiction show a variety of psychological, social and
interpersonal factors that also contribute quite clearly to drug
addiction – group pressures and availability of drugs, lower
self-esteem, perceived lack of opportunity for achievement
– factors that could never apply to rats, especially those in
the special circumstances of the laboratory cage. (Although,
come to think of it, this is probably the very reason they
like the drugs so much: the boredom of imprisonment,
curtailing of opportunity to lead a fulfilling life, cut-off from
family and friends.) Both these approaches to the study of
human addiction – the sociological and the neurological – are
deemed valid. But only one area of study – the neurological
– is viewed as applying in both cases. While it is evident
that humans and rats have similar brains, their social
behaviours are not so comparable. Participant observation
– common to studies of humans – has yet to be achieved
with rats and mice but I can confirm that it is only humans
who have dealers which supply them Class A drugs. (The
rats rely on research students.) This then strengthens the
neurobiological arguments for this field to the extent that
the social, collective factors become too vague or even trivial
in comparison.

The irony of this position is that information about the least
distinctively human aspect of ourselves (our brain neurology
and the behaviour of neurotransmitters which is all rather

similar in most mammals) – derived from studies using animals quite unlike human beings in general – becomes a powerful explanation of a human behavioural activity. But this says nothing about what makes a human being. At the level of brain neurobiology and addiction we are no longer distinctively human, we are clearly rat-like. This is known as biological reductionism – reducing humanness to its biological baseline which, in the end, results in a reduction of anything human to what is held in common with an animal. At the brain level, an approach to preventing or curing drug addiction may well be reasoned along parallel lines in rats and in humans. But at the level of the actual life of the organism, there are so many differences that this sole approach would be absurd. *It is the differences* – social, collective and cultural – *and not the neurological similarities that are important* when it comes to thinking about human being and human nature.

Despite this seemingly obvious conclusion about human nature, there have been some very persuasive ideas and dominant hypotheses that amount to an inaccurate blurring of our human being and the biology we humans share with other animals. A major paradigm or perspective that influences such a distortion arose halfway through the nineteenth century. This particular way of seeing things has permeated more aspects of the 'nature' of our human being than anything since (and that would include the Human Genome Project). I am referring, of course, to the theory of the evolution of species.

The theory of evolution, most commonly associated with Charles Darwin, grew from a number of investigations, discoveries and rediscoveries long before the work on inherited characteristics mapped by the Czech monk Mendel got revived. It took many more years before the modern study of genetics and DNA confirmed the mechanisms of inheritance in organisms. Darwin's original puzzle was how come there were so many species of organism in the world? Why were some similar but with clear variations and others clearly distinct from each other? And why were they found to be living where they were? This is not to mention why some who had once lived – judging from the fossil record – no longer existed in the present day; was there any connection between the extinct creatures and those alive today? European travellers over the 500 years prior to Darwin had brought back descriptions of creatures – such as the giraffe, elephant and rhinoceros – fabulously different to anything known in Europe where the people writing about such things lived. The creatures had, of course, been known about for millennia by the humans of their indigenous lands. The European travellers had also noticed creatures such as the zebra, for example, that looked similar to animals they were familiar with (in this case the horse) but which differed in particular aspects. These travellers also encountered groups of humans, which they found to vary from the European norm of how a human being was expected to appear and behave; the 'history' of *who* has decided what is human is developed at length in Chapter 7.[5]

Theories of evolution as anything other than armchair speculation were boosted into the realms of empirical possibility via discoveries unearthed by the new proto-science of geology – the *logos*, or knowledge, of the Earth's rocky crust. New technological developments in mining had been necessary for the exploitation of fuel and minerals that stoked the Industrial Revolution of the late eighteenth century. Thoughtful amateurs with time on their hands – often the owners of the mining land, or their sons – took up the idea of examining below the surface of the earth. In the rock strata they found a record of organic life on Earth compressed and preserved as fossilised remains. Because these remains appeared to date back to the beginnings of life on Earth, such discoveries paved the way for a dismissal of biblical theories of creation and the Garden of Eden. For the Victorians, this was the culmination of Enlightenment science based on human reason expressed as – and justified through – objective scientific rationalism. Or so it was thought. In Chapter 9, I examine the degree to which the evolutionists' dismissal of the creation myth merely constituted another myth – the myth of evolutionary science.

In the mid-nineteenth century, the Darwin-Wallace investigation into the variety and origin of species was leading to the conclusion that these species had arisen from common ancestors through a process of evolution and were not created *sui generis* by the Seventh Day or saved from extinction by Noah in a 'second creation' as the Bible said. Moreover, Darwin spelled out how species originated through a process of natural selection governed by how well each generation survived in their particular environmental niche. Those that had the best adapted qualities to survive and breed under their particular conditions – desert, forest, heat or cold – were the species that continued and were to be found in the present day. The theory deepened when it came to the mutation and retention of qualities like the neck of the giraffe and the skin of the rhino; these had to be explained for their successful adaptive qualities that accounted for their present existence. The simple idea was that the qualities animals showed – long necks or webbed feet – had persisted because these qualities were optimally fitted to the environmental niche or circumstances in which the creatures lived.

This explanation of the origin of species not only used evidence from field trips such as Darwin's to the Galapagos Islands but also cited the geological fossil record of organisms that no longer existed. It was reasoned that these constituted the ancestors of living organisms; by studying the fossils, further evidence for the process of natural selection might, up to a point, be found in a sequence of evolutionary development as judged from the fossil remains. The theory of evolution suggested that, eventually, a common ancestor responsible for a variety of present-day species may be detected by such methods.

By the logic of the day (and this is still the logic today), Darwin's theories extended to a claim that what was true for animal species must be true for the human species. Yes, you heard it right, *humans were henceforth regarded as simply another species*. This stands as the pinnacle of Enlightenment scientific reason where the aim all along had been the disenchantment and demystification of knowledge away from superstition and reliance on religious views. Through the application of a purely human, and thus unassailable, reason, the idea that all phenomena – whether inorganic, organic, animal or human – came into existence due to the Will of God who created it was, in educated circles, now dismissed. What shocked the Victorians who had placed such trust in the power of human beings to understand, conquer and exploit nature for their own benefit through the power of their rational mind was this: rationally explained by the science of evolution, human beings, it seems, had evolved from apes! Scientific fact! Such was the irony of celebrating human reason above all else.

This single idea is the source of that contradiction about ourselves I highlighted some pages back. The very creatures who have been able to work out how come things are like they are now, including why they themselves are as they are, discover in the process that they are in fact the evolved product of those other organisms they regularly use to confirm and define their own human uniqueness. Far from being a Victorian mistake in thinking, ridiculed and surpassed in the contemporary era – like the belief in physical harm brought about by masturbation, or the justification of hunting Aboriginal Australians to death through a denial of their humanness – this primate-based description of what it is to be a human being persists to this day.

It is over 150 years since Darwin published his seminal work and his ideas are remarkably robust in shaping our view of ourselves today. Since then there have been cool twists such as the way in which skeletal remains regarded as those of our earliest hominid ancestor were named 'Lucy'. This is no fancy Latin epithet like *Trigonia*[6] but arises simply because the palaeontologist who found 'her' was listening to the Beatles' song 'Lucy in the Sky with Diamonds' later that night. I guess this says something in general about the articulation of biology, psychology, science and popular culture which is very much where this present book is at. But what might be said specifically about such an articulation? A lighter approach to this business of Enlightenment scientific rationality and all its hubris? Maybe. Or, at the very least, an admission that naming something can be pretty random and it's not going to matter that much in the long run. Or, is it that once you have heard how a name has been arrived at, the gravity and the authority of the 'science' involved is put into human perspective? And that might be what this is all about. Not human nature, or even human being, but *human perspective*.

This brief introduction going from *Blade Runner* through human infant vulnerability to animal experiments and the assumptions of evolutionary theory, suggests how any thinking about our human being must involve cultural implications over and above the biological. From this arises the idea that one distinctive quality of a human being human is expressed in our capacity for *being in relationship with each other*. This aspect of human being has persisted since Aristotle's emphasis on humans having their being in community – and hence our 'political being'.[7] The latest observational studies of the human infant's instinctive, or archetypal, seeking of relationship no longer permit us to regard such behaviour along reductive, biological lines simply as a function for survival. It now seems much more likely that *relationship with others – for its own sake – is an embedded activity of humans through which they have their being*.[8] This is a theme that will become apparent from the many approaches this book takes to the subject of human being. To an important extent, the idea of each individual living to fulfil their own unique creative potential[9] must include an equal fulfilment of their *communal* being as members of shared cultures. Differences between human cultural groups in language, concepts and meanings found across the world can seem vast. As we have heard, the Nuer believe that human twins are birds. Western scientists believe that aspects of being human that are governed by groups of chemicals they call 'genes' can be discovered by looking at the lives of identical twins. Millions of families gather round a box-shaped invention that reveals images broadcast from thousands of miles away, while elsewhere families gather round a fire telling stories to each other. For human beings, being fully oneself means being fully human, which means being fully engaged with others. Individual life and cultural life are two sides of the same coin.

This introduction has expanded some of the angles we might expect to encounter in pursuit of questions concerning our human *being* as opposed to our human *nature*. All attempts to answer such questions directly seem impossible. Like the eye looking at itself, we are at a profound disadvantage. What I offer in the following chapters are reflections on the concerns, perspectives, strategies and reactions human beings experience while finding themselves as just one of thousands of living organisms in this world. The narratives and discussions here range from the way in which we conceive of the world using categories of opposites (Chapter 2), to the contradictory way we construct rules of behaviour called ethics as both protection and empowerment, as discussed in Chapter 4. Before this chapter I pave the way by considering the tricky play of power, influence and healing in Chapter 3. A further approach to the contradictions of being human continues in Chapter 5, which looks at the tendency in psychotherapy and in wider culture to abandon the intellect in favour of the emotions.

All the while I am keen to explore whether we have conceived our sense of human being similarly or very differently across the ages. Chapter 6 looks at this through considerations of what we know about matter from sub-atomic physics and how this affects our view of the mind and our perception of the world. What might look like a historical approach but one which seeks to undermine the assumptions we call 'history' is Chapter 7, where I link ideas humans have held about 'racial' difference to a particular style of consciousness which emerged in European cultures after the medieval era. This trend towards a split consciousness proved advantageous for the exploitation of natural resources and indigenous peoples, but has resulted in a form of human being divided against itself on both the individual and cultural level.

Many of the following chapters reflect on our human being human through contradictions such as those around the 'human' and the 'animal' which we encountered at the beginning of this introduction. For me, one of our key contradictions as human beings is the experience of both a conscious and an unconscious mind, and how this characterises us at the same time as it reveals us to ourselves. It would be simplistic to believe I am taking this approach because I am a psychotherapist and analyst with an anthropological and Jungian background. It strikes me that it is the other way round. The work I do, whether as a psychotherapist or as a film-maker or a writer is the expression of my own human being at this time as it arises from my personality and experience of life so far. In the same way, my other activities as a father, a lover, a traveller, enjoying music, films and the company of others are further expressions of this being. Ever since I can remember I have wanted to find out, create something and think about why human beings are as they are individually and collectively, with all their similarities and differences. All my activity, my being, contributes to this project. This book is the result of the writing activity. Further facets appear in the way I like to use characters and narratives from films to illustrate some points, as with *The Navigator: A Medieval Odyssey* (dir. V. Ward, 1988) in Chapter 6 and *Groundhog Day* (dir. H. Ramis, 1993) in Chapter 9. I consider the personal and cultural importance of movies themselves when I talk about Jean Cocteau's *Orphee* (1950) in Chapter 10. Following 'history' in Chapter 7, and memory and trauma in Chapter 8, 'time' becomes the focus in the last third of the book. Although a sense of human time has been hovering around from the beginning, Chapter 11 discusses, among other things, photography, movies and other late nineteenth-century inventions and the role they played in the shift in our modern experience of time.

Throughout the book you will notice short 'panel' pieces which are more or less linked to each following chapter. Like a movie short, these can be enjoyed as further reflections on the content of each chapter or as stand-alone pieces. Together with the photographs, they supply a more personal perspective on the theme of human being in all the ways it expresses itself.

The last chapter approaches the subject of death: the end of our being. Although I give small examples of how humans make and express meaning in their lives throughout the book, this last chapter, about a young child confronting a life-threatening illness, offers a 'live' version of ideas that have appeared in more abstract form elsewhere. By including visual images along with the narrative, his being is brought alive similar to the way in which a completed film soars beyond its beginnings as a screenplay. This direct way of bringing human being to life at the end of the book helps balance all those unavoidable, indirect – and often less satisfying – paths which have been necessary to the exploration of our human being.

Maybe through this child's story in the last chapter the question of what is human can be grasped in a less conscious fashion, out of the corner of one's eye, so to speak. Remember, all this is about *your* human being as well. You as a reading being are essential to everything that is going on in these pages. When the great film editor Walter Murch talks about what happens with an audience watching a movie he uses the analogy of the vacuum tube found in an amplifier. Power in the form of electricity comes into the tube as a powerful but unorganised current; at the same time music comes in as an intelligent and coherent (organised) but weak current. They get combined to produce the powerful coherence that pushes the speaker cone which we hear as music. In a movie theatre, the film supplies the coherence; the power is coming not from the film – or, in this case, from anything in this book – 'It's coming from the collective lives and emotional world of the audience ... a tremendously powerful but unorganised force that is looking for coherence ... what is really getting them to leave home [to go to the cinema] is a temporary dissatisfaction with where they are, craving something that will cohere them, at least temporarily, within the self and with a bunch of like-minded people.'[10] I am using Murch's example of the relationship between the coherence of the film and the power of the audience as a further analogy for the relationship between this book and you. I have no idea how 'coherent' this book may be, but I do know that it can only have its being through the power brought to it by you, its readers.

It will be up to you how it is read. Perhaps you will start with the last chapter and read the book in reverse. I don't know. Maybe, after looking at this introduction – standing in the bookshop or sitting in the library, still deciding – you will not read the book at all. Whatever you decide – and that includes changing your mind as many times as you wish – I offer these words and thoughts that follow as a celebration of all our human being. Mine and yours. Then and now.

Notes

1 Gray, John ([1948] 2002) *Straw Dogs: Thoughts on Humans and Other Animals*. London: Granta, p. 58.

2 Williams, Don (2001) 'If you could see what I've seen with your eyes . . . ' Post-human psychology and *Blade Runner*, in Hauke, C. & Alister, I. (eds) *Jung and Film, Post-Jungian Takes on the Moving Image*. Hove: Brunner-Routledge, pp. 110–28.

3 Evans-Pritchard, p.113; quoted by Gellner in 'Concepts and society': pp. 34–5 of Wilson, B.R. (ed.) ([1970] 1981) *Rationality*. Oxford: Blackwell.

4 On another note, some previous generations of parents have in fact regarded human infants as more animal than human and have used swaddling practices – to keep babies in upright positions and deter the crawling stage regarded as too animal-like and insufficiently human – until children were able to walk upright. From Gottlieb, B. (1993) *The Family in the Western World from the Black Death to the Industrial Age*. New York: Oxford University Press, pp. 134–42.

5 For an amusing and succinct summary of the European treatment of native peoples try Randy Newman's song 'Great Nations of Europe' from his CD *Bad Love* (1999), Dreamworks Records. It says it all in about three minutes.

6 That's a clam to you and me. As in *Trigonia Chowder*.
7 When it comes to finding this in our own psychology, Andrew Samuels makes a fine contribution in his books, *The Political Psyche* (1993) (London: Routledge) and *Politics on The Couch* (2002) (London: Polity). Kenan Malik (2000) *Man, Beast and Zombie: What Science Can and Cannot Tell Us About Human Nature* (London: Weidenfeld & Nicolson), is also an excellent read and does just what it says on the cover.
8 I will refer you to Stern, Daniel N. (1985) *The Interpersonal World of the Infant: A View from Psychoanalysis and Developmental Psychology* (New York: Basic Books), as a good place to start looking at how psychologists are understanding the way humans do not have to 'learn' or 'acquire' the capacity for relationship in early life but bring this with them at birth.
9 Which is not only found particularly in C.G. Jung's psychological concept of individuation but is also an approach to life valued in contemporary western society as a whole.
10 Walter Murch quoted by Koppelman, C. (2005) in *Behind the Seen: How Walter Murch Edited Cold Mountain using Apple's Final Cut Pro and what this Means for Cinema*. Berkeley, CA: New Riders/Peachpit, p. 19.

Siena

Sometimes, some places can have an extraordinary effect on us. These unpredictable effects surprise us with their intensity and leave us puzzling 'Why this?' and 'Why now?' I remember a time when I was travelling in Italy with my friend David Peat. We had been at a conference in Assisi, itself a magical place, and we were on our way by bus to Pari, the village where David and his wife live. The first bus took us to Siena and we had over an hour's wait there before our connection took us on the final leg of our journey. David knew Siena well so he decided to wait in a shady café while I had a look at the city, which I had never visited before. It was a very hot day in late summer and the famous horse-race that has been run on the Campo in the centre of town for hundreds of years had taken place the day before. The Campo is an oval 'town square' at the heart of Siena which is approached from the neighbouring streets via archways with a number of steps going down. As I descended towards the Campo a group of young people were walking around the edge of the Campo with coloured ribbons round their necks. From one or two of these hung a baby's feeding bottle and on others was a baby's dummy (or 'pacifier'). The marchers were singing and celebrating so I guessed they might be to do with the winning horse and the town district it represented, but I had no idea about the bottles and the dummies.

However, my interest in these was completely eclipsed by what I felt once I had reached the bottom of the steps and gazed at the Campo, which stretched in front of me and to both sides. I was immediately overwhelmed by a feeling of familiarity, just like when returning home after a long absence, or revisiting a house once lived in when young. Not only was this feeling of the familiar quite surprising as I had never seen this place before, but so too was the intensity of nostalgia I felt. With my eyes brimming with tears I walked diagonally across the Campo to an area on my right, noting a rectangular fountain affair which I was certain had not been there in 'my day'. The fountain was indeed more recent: it dated from the early eighteenth century.

Figure 1.1 The Campo, Siena

Once I reached the far side of the Campo (to the right of the town hall as you face it), I steadied myself on a post and, still full of tears, gazed across to the other side. Going in a semicircle, the buildings curve round the oval and are several stories high with shops and restaurants at the bottom with their huge terracotta blinds spread to shade their customers. From nowhere, the words came to me: 'Those are our shops'. Although my rational self was fully aware that I had never been here before, at the same time another part of me was experiencing the feelings of someone returning home. The phrase 'Those are our shops' added a greater sense of intimate *familias* as if, indeed, I had belonged to a family who had owned and worked the shops I was gazing at. When or how, I could not say.

There is nothing rational that can be said about the experience, no way to explain it. Others may be tempted to understand my emotional response and the words I 'heard' as a type of reincarnation experience: the idea that I had lived a human life in this place in medieval times. But I have never before had any affinity for Italy or Siena, its language or even its food, over and above other places I have visited. If reincarnation 'explains' my reaction, it is rather a one-off example. I was still in analysis at the time and in talking over the Siena experience the best we could get to was that I had somehow been sensitive to and tapped into the thousands of years of human activity, passion, love and belonging the place must hold.

Vague though it is, perhaps that is the answer. I met up with David at the café and we boarded the bus to Pari. There was a young Italian woman sitting in front of us and I could hear she spoke English. I asked her about the babies bottles and the dummies on ribbons around the necks of the marchers. 'Those were their colours; they come from the district whose rider and horse won the Campo yesterday. They were celebrating again. It is a very important event. When your horse wins, it is like a new baby has been born.'

2

Thinking in opposites

When I was being taught English language in junior school in the 1950s, a favourite exercise was the completion of a list of "opposites". Down one side of the blackboard the teacher would write a number of words such as HOT, DAY, BLACK, and so on, while we pupils had to offer the opposite to these – COLD, NIGHT, WHITE and so on. The pairs would start simple enough but we would soon come up against more problematic categories. With ANIMAL for instance, what was the opposite to be? Was it HUMAN? Or should it be BIRD or even, INSECT? And while WET was obviously the opposite of DRY, with very little between them – after all, DAMP is still on the wet side – was FIRE really the 'opposite' of WATER? Or was SUN really the "opposite" of MOON? Or MAN the 'opposite' of WOMAN? As soon as you start to look into this, opposites are not always what they seem to be.

Having said this, however, it is possible to detect certain areas of experience – and ways of categorising such experience – which consistently produce opposites that seem to be universal for humans everywhere. One of these seems to be *spatial categories*. The way we refer to positions in three-dimensional space seems to be governed by opposites that we regard as unambiguous: UP/DOWN, NORTH/SOUTH, WEST/EAST, ABOVE/BELOW, LEFT/RIGHT, INSIDE/OUTSIDE and so on. That is not to deny that any of these may be relative. If I am already positioned in a place you refer to as UP, then your UP will be 'my' DOWN. These categories of opposites seem like common sense because that is exactly why we have them. They derive from our sensory, mostly visual, perception of the world and when rendered as words they help us communicate our sensory and bodily orientation to ourselves and to each other. There is another range of opposites that might lead us into affirming that there are 'real' and unalterable opposites in nature. Again we start from the human senses and the limitations imposed by biology. It is a fact that when we stare at a red-coloured patch for a while, when we look away we are left with an afterimage that is green. Similarly, staring at a blue patch leaves an afterimage of yellow. RED/GREEN and BLUE/YELLOW seem to be biologically governed opposites. We do not choose these opposites, but we *do choose how we name them*.

However, there are other pairs of opposites also derived from the senses we have in common which, although they seem as fundamental as those just mentioned, do not follow from the human body's need to orientate itself in space, but from more arbitrary pairings of concepts. Here I am thinking of SUN/MOON, NIGHT/DAY, EARTH/SKY, FIRE/WATER, LAND/SEA, SUMMER/WINTER and so on. Why should the sun be the 'opposite' of the moon? If we lived on a planet where there were three moons in the night sky with only one sun in the daytime, would we still be as ready to place sun and moon in opposition? And while earth and sky seem an obvious contrast, as do land and sea and summer and winter, and provide very contrasting experiences for us as human beings, they seem to be more arbitrary when it comes to making them opposites. Their oppositional nature again derives from human needs and interests, but they are a step away from the spatial and 'biological' opposites mentioned above. That phrase 'human needs and interests' is one to remember and one to which we shall return when we discuss the psychology of opposites.

The fundamental sensory experiences of heat and cold, and of light and dark, which our bodies and our senses are particularly sensitive to, tend to form a basis for human psychology to polarise experience as a way of understanding, ultimately manipulating the world for human ends. Such a 'manipulating' of our experience, mediated through our psychology, the activity of the mind, results in human *culture*. Human psychology may well be universal through all places and all times, but the forms it takes, the way it expresses itself, these are cultural. Psychology and culture are intrinsically linked; there is very little to be found in the world of human beings that is not mediated by the cultural form which it takes. The same blood may flow in the veins of all humans at all times and places, but the meaning assigned to that blood, what it might signify from one group to another and from one occasion to another, will vary greatly. At one moment blood may be consumed as a way of participating in the strength of a warrior, another time it may be spilt to appease a higher being or 'god', and on a further occasion it may be the tabooed substance that signifies a woman's menses. In the human world, BLOOD is never simply blood. It is always 'blood' in inverted commas.

So it is in a similar fashion that all 'fundamentals' of human experience need to be understood. This includes the 'opposites' that seem to be so fundamental to our human experience. All our polarities, from MAN/WOMAN through to SUN/MOON, HILL/VALLEY, HOT/COLD, LEFT/RIGHT and even RED/GREEN, or abstracts like PRESENCE/ABSENCE, all of these are not so much funda-mental 'truths' about phenomena, as they are ways in which the human mind creates meaning for itself. Out of that 'blooming bursting confusion' of experience as the psycho-analyst Michael Balint once called it when talking about the impact of the world on the senses of a human infant, humans make meaningful sense of their experience.[1] That 'sense' develops not only as conscious knowledge of the world, but also in the unconscious psyche. The opposites are an important way in which the psyche 'knows' the world. But more importantly, rather than simply a way in which human psychology structures experience in a more or less conscious fashion, polarities and oppositional 'thinking' also seem to be the conditions within which the human psyche encounters reality and creates meaning.

C.G. Jung and the opposites

Of all the great psychologists of recent times, it is C.G. Jung who has drawn our attention to the significance of opposites when it comes to understanding the human psyche. My own path that led me to train as an analyst and psychotherapist within the Jungian tradition did not stem from medicine or from psychoanalysis for that matter. A while before, I had taken a university degree in psychology and social anthropology which provided an excellent foundation. My interest in Jung, however, lay further back in my youth when I had studied and practised a good deal of Buddhism, especially its Zen variation, and been influenced by the Taoist literature of Lao Tse and Chuang Tzu. Through these texts – and those of modern commentators such as Alan Watts, Thomas Merton, D.T. Suzuki and others – I discovered the idea that western thinking is dualistic and tends to construct reality in oppositional terms: an 'either/or' way of thinking. By contrast, the thinking of eastern philosophies was directing us towards the 'non-dual' – a way of knowing the reality of the world and our human existence that did not rely on the dualistic thinking of the West. To a young man puzzled and troubled by the awareness of 'both sides of the problem' – God/no God or selfishness/self-sacrifice being typical moral dilemmas – it came as a great relief to know that such a non-dual point of view existed or had at least been conceived. Achieving that point of view for oneself was quite another matter entirely. That was the way of the Bodhisattva, the enlightened human who then returns to the cycle of rebirth and death rather than leaving this world for the non-dual realm of nirvana. As a man educated and absorbed into the cultural atmosphere of late twentieth-century western thinking, there was no easy way out of my dualistic approach to myself and existence. It was, and is, basic to the psychological style of psyche that typifies the western mind. Jung realised this, but at the same time he became very familiar with the writings and interpreters of Eastern thought, and he developed a psychology, a theory of the western mind that takes account of both positions. In doing so he does not attempt to escape the dualistic thinking of the West – the opposition of 'East' and 'West' is, after all, typical of this very phenomena – but instead, Jung developed a phenomenology of Western psychology that both takes account of the opposites and also points out how we are also able to *transcend* them.

The psychological approach Jung developed did not try to bring West and East together – in fact he strongly recommended that Eastern thinking is not for the West as the East developed its consciousness of such matters a thousand years ahead of us. The Eastern way is not suited to Western conditions, Jung states.[2] What is preferred is a way to understand ourselves which addresses the dualistic, opposites-making Western psyche in its own terms without need to translate these into Eastern concepts. This is not to deny that comparisons can be made between Jung's psychology and elements of Eastern philosophy, and he wrote many commentaries to that effect in introductions to books by Suzuki on Zen and by Richard Wilhelm on Chinese philosophy.[3] But the crucial aspect of Jung's psychology is how it is rooted in what I have just referred to as *phenomenology*. In other words, Jung's ideas arise not from philosophical or metaphysical speculations – although many mistake them as such – but from him observing the phenomena of the human psyche or mind and the way humans make meaning for themselves. Jung found this not only in the dreams and fantasies of his patients on the psychiatric ward or in his consulting room, but also in the beliefs, myths and rituals of non-Western societies, and in ancient texts of Gnosticism and alchemy.

The psychology of Freud and Jung

The thinkers of the Enlightenment had no need for the notion of an 'unconscious' mind. Consciousness and, above all, *reason*, were the qualities that placed human beings above all other creatures and eventually next to God – by knowing His mind through the study of science. Freud's psycho-analytic theory asserted the importance of another 'mind' in 'man' – the *unconscious* – and thereby rediscovered and reaffirmed a dualism in humans and their psychology. Interestingly, the prevailing dualistic idea – the absolute distinction of mind and body, the so-called Cartesian split that had dominated western Enlightenment thinking – seemed to be challenged by the new dualism of the conscious and unconscious psyche. This can be seen in the way that Freud developed his psychoanalytic theory by treating the physical symptoms of female hysteric patients. He found that their physical symptoms – partial paralysis, anaesthesia, squint, hydrophobia (aversion to water) – did not have any organic, body-based cause, but persisted as the result of psychological trauma and defences. By addressing the mental or psychological state through the techniques of talking, free association and interpretation, Freud claimed to remove the physical symptoms. Mind and body were seen to be far from separate after all – a commonplace observation these days – but this 'discovery' led to a new dualism that was to prove a powerful influence in the way the Western mind conceived itself. This was the 'new' pair of opposites: the conscious and the unconscious mind.

In classic psychoanalytic theory, there are further oppo-sites. *Ego* (*das Ich* – the 'I') is the centre of consciousness, the aspect of mind that deals with the perceptions and reality of the 'outside' world. It also mediates our knowledge of our inner world of cognitions, emotions and fantasy. The *id* (*das Es* – the 'It') refers to that part of the mental structure where the passions, the instincts and all that is 'less human' in the sense of 'less civilised' dwell. It is Freud's view that humans became civilised – and thus began human culture – through the continuing repression of the forces stemming from the id, but the price we have had to pay for this – some more steeply than others – is our neurosis. According to Freud we should be tolerant of our 'common unhappiness' (once psycho-analytic treatment has removed our 'neurotic misery') as this is the price of and the foundation of our 'success' as civilised human beings.

Jung's view of the psyche differs from Freud's in several important ways. Some of these differences – such as his denial that psychic energy or libido was purely sexual, and denial of the importance of Freud's Oedipal theory of personality development – are not so central to our theme of opposites and polarity. Therefore I will restrict this chapter to the differences most revealing of a human tendency to oppositional thinking.

In Jung's psychology, the unconscious is not merely a negative and primitive aspect of the psyche that has to be repressed for civilisation to exist, but it is also the source of our creativity and the ground of our fullest expression as human beings. It follows from this that attention to the unconscious, which began in the late nineteenth century and characterised the twentieth century as a way in which we think about ourselves, amounts to something different for Jung. In an era which is characterised by an overemphasis on consciousness, rationality, and the valuation of intellectual and instrumental applications of the mind to 'conquer' the world of nature, Jung's genius was to present the uncon-scious as the complementary opposite to consciousness – an aspect of psyche which we ignore at our peril. It is the Otherness of the unconscious that interests Jung and should interest us in our pursuit of a fuller humanity, both indi-vidually and collectively. Jung called this pursuit the path of *individuation* – the path to becoming who one truly is, to the fulfilling of one's potential, or 'becoming who you are'. For Jung this is not only an individual need but is also a vital need for contemporary western culture overall. As he once said in an interview:

Nowadays, the world hangs by a thin thread, and that thread is the psyche of man . . . *We* are the great danger. The psyche is the great danger. What if something goes wrong with the psyche? . . . how important it is to know something about it? But we know nothing about it? Nobody would give credit to the idea that the psychic processes of the ordinary man have any importance whatever.[4]

What Jung is referring to – and what he thought his psychology and treatment method could help with – is the way that the psyche of human beings in the developed, industrial countries (and that is just about everywhere these days in our global economy, but centrally meaning Europe and the USA) has progressively suffered an impoverishment since the dominance of a certain one-sided consciousness was ushered in with the Enlightenment. Unlike Freud, the repression of the unconscious for Jung is a lack and a loss, and one which ultimately threatens human life on the planet. These days we find this criticism expressed practically in many areas of concern and lobbying, such as Green politics with its concern for world ecology and the potential hazards involved in new scientific techniques such as GM crops, among several examples.

Jung finds that contemporary consciousness suffers from an over-reliance on oppositional thinking: *either* Democrat *or* Republican, Right wing *or* Left wing views, *either* truth in science *or* falsehood. Even the very concepts of conscious and unconscious stem from the same discourse of polarity. But that does not mean that these concepts may not also serve as the very ideas that Jungian psychology uses to deconstruct and critique such essentialist views. If consciousness sees things in a hierarchy where one side of the opposing pair is always favoured, then the unconscious is the 'place' where the Other resides – not simply the Other as yet another opposition, but perhaps the Other to the very problem of polarising, oppositional positions themselves.

A useful way of illustrating what I mean is to take the case of the oppositional categories MALE and FEMALE the gen-derised pairing of the *masculine* and the *feminine*. Not only did Jung believe that the sexes 'represent a supreme pair of opposites, not hopelessly divided by logical contradiction, but, because of the mutual attraction between them, giving promise of union and actually making it possible'[5] but also, for Jung and many other thinkers, contemporary conscious-ness is dominated by a particular style of rationality that may be classed as 'masculine'. This refers to the active, pene-trating, linear, directive, focused mode of rationality that characterises our science, our economics and our politics. We live in what is referred to as a patriarchal society, where masculine values and styles of consciousness prevail; the dominant consciousness is patriarchal and masculine. Over the last thirty or forty years, in politics and then wide-spread throughout our Western culture, a counterbalance has been sought in terms of the *feminine*. In practical terms this has occurred via the lobbying and publications of the Women's Movement which sought greater equality of oppor-tunities and fairness for actual women and girls; but this concrete expression of the struggle between the 'opposites' of male and female points us towards something rather deeper. If the dominant consciousness 'is' male, then, as the Other to consciousness and in Jungian terms, the unconscious has been characterised as female. It follows therefore, that as we are witnessing a social revolution in terms of the positions of men and women and, most importantly, the revaluing of so-called masculine and feminine approaches and traits in the 'outer' world, what this also means is that the psyche is being required to address the one-sidedness of consciousness and integrate the unconscious in psycho-logical, and perhaps spiritual, terms.

Following ancient ideas like those of Heraclites, Jung believed that psyche and life itself derived energy from the interplay of opposites. This means that psyche suffers when matters become too one-sided, like in the example of consciousness dominated by a masculinist style of ratio-nality just mentioned. Psyche will produce compensatory phenomena, just as our dreams produce imagery that compensates and tries to strike a balance with our conscious experience. Thus the attention paid to the feminine in the late twentieth century was a psychic compensation we should take most seriously. It is not enough to treat it as a surface phenomenon of a merely ideological, economic or political kind without seeing that all these categories rest on something much deeper. Gender opposites have been around for time immemorial as a typical form for denoting difference found throughout humanity. Closely connected with sexuality and with the different anatomy of men and women, opposites such as ACTIVITY/PASSIVITY, PRESENCE/ ABSENCE, INWARD/OUTWARD and so on have produced metaphors along gender lines. The contemporary post-Jungian, and postmodern shift that we are now experiencing in the way that so-called 'feminine' qualities are being revalued and integrated with the dominant 'masculine' consciousness heralds a psychological shift on several levels. And this should not be regarded as some final move of reconciliation or 'cure' for Western culture or the Western psyche either. It is rather a living example of psyche at work. As Jung reminds us: 'The meaning and purpose of a problem seems to be not in its solution, but in our working at it incessantly. This alone preserves us from stultification and petrifaction.'[6]

Jung notes: 'Life, being an energic process, needs the opposites, for without opposition there is, as we know, no energy.'[7] The opposites throughout human life, the psyche and nature in general seem to be a vital way of understanding the energy and motion of existence – in all these forms – itself. I mentioned above that Jung's term for the psychic and overall development of individuals was individuation. From what I have said I think you can see how this inherent quality of all being to *become itself* would also apply to human cultural life. After all, this too is part of 'nature'. The opposites seem to be part of this movement. Whether couched in the metaphor of masculine and feminine, the confrontation and the integration of the unconscious and the conscious psyche

'. . . means open conflict and open collaboration at once. That, evidently is the way human life should be. It is the old game of hammer and anvil: between them the patient iron is forged into an indestructible whole, an "individual".'[8]

Notes

1 Balint, M. (1952) *Primary Love and Psychoanalytic Technique*, London: Hogarth and Balint, M. (1968) *The Basic Fault: Therapeutic Aspects of Regression*. London: Tavistock.
2 Jung, C.G. (1936) Yoga and the West, in *Collected Works*, Vol. 11, *Psychology and Religion: West and East*. London: Routledge & Kegan Paul, paras 859–76.
3 To be found in Jung, C.G. ([1958] 1981) *Collected Works*, Vol. 11, *Psychology and Religion: West and East*. London: Routledge & Kegan Paul.
4 Jung, C.G. (1957) quoted in W. McGuire and R.F.C. Hull (eds) (1980) *C.G. Jung Speaking: Interviews and Encounters*. London: Picador, p. 288.
5 Jung, C.G. (1959) *Collected Works*, Vol. 9ii, *Aion. Researches into the Phenomenology of the Self*. London: Routledge & Kegan Paul, para. 425.
6 Jung, C.G. ([1931] 1969) *Collected Works*, Vol. 8, *The Structure and Dynamics of the Psyche*. London: Routledge & Kegan Paul, para. 771.
7 Jung, C.G. ([1948] 1981) *Collected Works*, Vol. 11, *Psychology and Religion: West and East*. London: Routledge & Kegan Paul, para. 291.
8 Jung, C.G. ([1940] 1959) *Collected Works*, Vol. 9i, *The Archetypes and the Collective Unconscious*. London: Routledge & Kegan Paul, para. 522.

The washing machine

Once, a man told me how, when he was very young, his mother used to sit him in front of the washing machine to keep him quiet. The clothes went round and round in the suds and the infant watched the window as they all swirled about. His mother then went about her chores confident the child was occupied. She was right. This little boy was intelligent and curious, but he had also learned it was best to do what mother says. His parents fed him, loved him, sometimes played with him and he was trusting that his mother knew what was good for him. So he watched the washing machine. He watched and wondered what he was meant to be seeing. He wondered what he was meant to be doing with this experience. But he kept watching. Because it had been presented to him in good faith by his trustworthy mother, he wanted to make sense of the washing machine. In the same way as if this was his first experience of a circus, or a train set, he applied his normal level of infant curiosity, interest and intelligence to watching the washing machine.

It will not surprise you to hear that later in life he came to discover many 'washing machines'. But now they took the form of a friend's huge over-concern with the health of her cat. Or it was a colleague's preference for an inconvenient and irrational way of running the office. On another occasion, this man found himself giving his full attention to someone else's mistake at the supermarket. Every time he would get drawn into someone else's particular situation as if he had a responsibility towards it and *as if he had chosen the situation himself*. Once he realised the connection and worked out what he was doing he was able to leave others' concerns where they belonged. He did not lack sympathy, but he became realistic about where his responsibility and interest ended and theirs began.

Our lives are surrounded by washing machines. Daily we may find ourselves in front of one, fascinated and involved until, if we are lucky, we wake up and find it is not our concern. Just because others present us with statements, problems or behaviours it does not mean they need automatically to command our attention. You did not ask to be there. Watch out for the times when you get plonked in front of the washing machine. Remember you can always get up, walk away and find something more interesting.

3

'Who's in charge here?' Knowledge, power and human being

At the end of the previous chapter I suggested that while we benefit from the interplay of energy between opposites, conscious thinking can create difficulties when one side becomes too firmly favoured over another. In such a hierarchy, the favoured side seeks to remain dominant. This brings us to a perennial theme of what it is to be human: human being as beliefs around and the enactment of power and knowledge – and the relationship between them. How do we proceed with this? Through politics? Through 'experts'? Through religion, science or what?

Michel Foucault, knowledge and power

When the French philosopher Michel Foucault began to map the state of western relationships between knowledge and power at the end of the 1960s in works such as *Madness and Civilisation* and *The Archaeology of Knowledge*,[1] he spent a great deal of time on psychiatry as the locus where these were well illustrated. And if psychiatry proved a fruitful example, the case of psychoanalytic therapy proved abundant when it came to the relations between knowledge and power. Foucault felt that the interweaving effects of power and knowledge could be 'grasped with greater certainty in the case of a science as 'dubious' as psychiatry.[2]

But Foucault does not simply mean the worst excesses of the political use of psychiatry, as in Stalin's USSR where thousands of individuals were sent to the gulags. In this case, knowledge and power took the form of a psychiatric 'diagnosis' which was used to condemn the views – and consequently the minds – of dissenters as insane because they did not support the Stalinist state.

More importantly, Foucault's analysis points out an important and subtle shift in the way power is conceived. In the USSR example, power was once thought of as judicial, repressive and negative – something that stopped freedom with a big 'No!' But Foucault makes it clear that, from the eighteenth century Enlightenment onward, power became the creative force to structure human populations in terms of their bodies, their sexuality, their norms of belief and their expectations and knowledge.[3] Therefore, power and its relationship with what we know (or are permitted or permit ourselves to know) is embedded in our sense of human being (what it is to be the man or woman or child that we are) in a far more subtle way.

'Repression' – which, after the idea of the unconscious itself, was *the* key concept introduced by psychoanalysis – is no longer sufficient as an explanation of the workings of power. Foucault reckons that repression alone could not work. On its own, the forbidding factor in our human affairs – whether in the form of being 'kept in our place', working for the master under feudal or slave conditions, or when repressing our sexual or acquisitive desires in Freud's broader picture of what makes us civilised – was not enough. 'If power were never anything but repressive, if it never did anything but to say no, do you really think one would be brought to obey it?' Foucault asks.[4]

> What makes power hold good . . . is simply the fact that it doesn't only weigh on us as a force that says no, but that it . . . produces things, it induces pleasure, forms knowledge, produces discourse. It must be considered as a productive network which runs through the whole

social body, much more than as a negative instance whose function is repression.[5]

In the key area of sexuality and repression Foucault points out that writings in the eighteenth century and onward which brought attention to the dangers of childhood sexuality and especially masturbation were most effective not as a discourse on forbidding and repression but as a more technical and positive exercise in power. Foucault concludes, 'The result was a sexualizing of the infantile body, a sexualizing of the bodily relationship between parent and child, a sexualizing of the familial domain. "Sexuality" is far more of a positive product of power than power was ever repression of sexuality.'[6]

A further illustration of the relationship between power and knowledge as understood by Freidrich Nietzsche is worth looking at. Not least because Foucault was much influenced by this philosopher's radical analysis of the modern western take on what it means to be a human being. Nietzsche points out how our sense of power and our sense of what is meaningful go together. We change our general perspectives – our knowledge of what is true, of what we can claim, what we can say – according to our need to retain meaning in our lives and thus maintain our sense of power. Nietzsche cites the case of Christianity, which he calls a 'slave morality'. Under conditions of domination by the Romans – in this case a real physical repression of one group by another using force and punishment of the body – Christians assigned new meanings to their subordinate position as a dominated group. By valorising the idea of further punishment in the concept of 'turning the other cheek', and exalting the position of the subordinated as in 'the meek shall inherit the earth', the Christian ethic succeeded in maintaining a sense of power by finding new meaning in the Christians' domination by the Romans. The example shows how the repression produced by a dominant force is not a sufficient explanation of power, and that the same power works creatively to assign new meanings for human beings who are always hungry to experience meaningfulness in their lives because it delivers them a *sense* of their own power.

Power and the construction of meaning

We have now hit upon some terms that bring us closer to the issue of power and knowledge in psychotherapy and analysis: not just *repression*, already much mentioned, but *meaningfulness* and the sense of one's own *potency*. These themes are clearly close to what many agree to be the aims of therapy. If I may speak in ideal terms: a client comes for help to a well-meaning, compassionate, interested psychotherapist who has been trained in accordance with a body of theory and who has undergone their own therapy so that they will be enabled to work with the client's material in a special way, minimally interrupted by their own interests and foibles of a more subjective nature. In other words, there is expected a degree of objectivity, expertise, skill in understanding the client and working with what arises in the relationship (including understanding by the therapist of their own reactions) and feeding this back to the client for the client's benefit.

You will notice that I have depicted a contemporary ideal picture of what we wish to achieve in therapy and what we train therapists for. I have not emphasised what many outside the profession and those of a historical inclination often assume, which is that the therapist or analyst takes a very blank, neutral stance to the client. Or the way in which the therapist is thought to be scrupulous in not divulging any personal information (including aspects of their personality), and to work with firm theoretical ideas, evidence of which the therapist expects to uncover in the client's material. By maintaining this regime, the therapist is then characterised as being confident of producing an objective assessment and analysis of the client's psychological position, which they will then deliver as interpretation and comment.

But, in the end, the 'soft' image and the 'hard' image of the therapist are not so very different. The apparently contrasting neutral, objective stance and the empathic, inter-subjective stance provide two roots to knowledge of the psyche that many therapists use. The trouble is that they both have this is common: they assume that the therapist *knows* and the client doesn't! Although there is little contemporary practice – I won't say none – featuring the classical Freudian cliché of a silent analyst sitting out of sight of a client who is instructed to let their words flow in free association while lying supine on a couch, there are several elements of this most in-egalitarian relationship between two people forever present in all psychotherapy.

When referring to this early model and the power of the analyst, Stephen Frosh makes a claim for the advances that Kleinian theory have brought to the development of psycho-analysis.[7] Frosh reckons that the way in which the object relations and Kleinian styles of therapy admit to the exchange of unconscious processing between therapist and client shows these theories and styles have a more egalitarian rela-tionship than the classical, distanced styles of analysis. The neutrality of therapists, which was originally emphasised to support a type of scientific 'objectivity' has resulted in a con-tradiction in the way it is now seen to contribute to definite inequalities of power between therapist and client, thus compromising 'objectivity'. The trouble with the apparent correction of this by Kleinian and object relations styles is that although unconscious processes are acknowledged as continuing in the therapist as well as the client, it is still the therapist who *knows* and the client who does not. Any challenge or confrontation by the client is still absorbed into a discourse that is structured on the asymmetry of an expert knowledge system. In other words, clients' comments about the therapist are nearly always absorbed into the theoretical perspective that says 'this is a projection' or the more pre-cisely expert comment that attributes the client's perspective to that highly specialised knowledge of *the transference*.

Let me offer an illustration. I know of an instance where a client was seeing a Kleinian therapist in a basement room next to a busy road and where the windows were kept shut to minimise noise. It was a hot day and the client asked for the windows to be opened. The therapist resisted this idea (meaning, he did not agree to do so but questioned what the client 'really' wanted) and so the client opened the window herself. The therapist was visibly aggravated by this challenge of autonomy yet proceeded to interpret the client's actions in terms of *her* aggressive feelings. Of course the client may well have had aggressive feelings towards the therapist in a transference sense or in a more real sense, before the incident. But in this example, it is the provocative behaviour of the therapist (in not taking the request as if it had any 'face-value' quality at all which it plainly did) that provokes the client's action, which may or may not have been initially aggressive at the time of the request (which would have seemed most reasonable in other non-therapy circum-stances). But given the theoretical importance of aggression and the emphasis on a non-gratifying, abstinent style in Kleinian work, the therapist seems to have manipulated a situation along the lines of Kleinian expectations in which the client had no say about her own motivations, let alone her choice to have the window opened! The client is denied the power her adult request would have brought in non-therapy contexts, and experiences her 'childlike' impotence while the therapist gets both theory and potency confirmed. But all of this arises out of the structural artificiality of the theory and technique of the therapeutic style which results in a position where, if meaning is to be found, it can only be the therapist's meaning.

The parental metaphor, in-egalitarian relationships and the power of the other

The maintenance of the power differential in therapy owes a good deal to the way in which the therapeutic relationship has been modelled on that of parent and child. I want to emphasise that this has not arisen the other way round. By which I mean that there is nothing 'natural' about seeing the therapist-client relationship in terms of a parent and child

– whether the parent is a father as in the earlier days of psychoanalysis, or a 'mother' as has been more common since Klein, Horney and Winnicott from the 1930s on. This metaphor of parent and child is one that is clearly suited to the in-egalitarian nature of the therapeutic relationship, and one which tends to support rather than challenge the power hierarchy. Moreover, this particular type of in-egalitarian relationship between parent and child – which we may characterise as paternalistic even when mothering qualities are imagined – derives from the general culture of a certain time and place (bourgeois Europe between 1900 and 1939) and is not necessarily a universal mode of relationships between parents and children. An in-egalitarian therapeutic practice emerging in a culture which already holds in-egalitarian power relations between its members – and especially between adults and children – is of course likely to find material that would supply such a metaphor.

However, over the last 15 or 20 years, the voice of actual children having a say in how they are cared for – their right to negotiate with adult carers rather than simply obey them – has been a growing trend in Europe and USA. Such a change will influence the metaphors used in psychotherapy, and when power inequalities between parents and children are not so clear, psychotherapy will either find a new metaphor, or, and this is far more likely, the power relationships in psychotherapy will themselves change along similar lines.[8]

What I am suggesting is that a practice like psychotherapy with its in-egalitarian power relationships will then seek a metaphorical description in another field of in-egalitarian relations that prevails in the same general culture. In our culture the parent-child relationship presents an opportunity for such comparison due to its similar power differentials in its present form. What both fields have most in common is their power differential which may manifest in factors such as dependency, idealisation, helplessness, greater knowledge, caring capacities, need to be understood and many others that may be cited in support of a parent-child metaphor as accurate for psychotherapy. This perspective also weakens any idea that we are dealing with more than a metaphor here and that somehow the therapeutic relationship is a repeat or reliving of the parent-child relationship. The crucial element is *the repeating of the in-egalitarian commonalities in both.*

And lastly, although I clearly do not support a view that says one field (psychotherapy) derives its relationship quality from another field (parent-child relationships), what I do say is that *both* fields are sensitive to cultural change and values and when these involve interpersonal matters, we may well witness parallel changes in these fields just as elsewhere in the culture.[9] But it would be ridiculous to support a parent-child metaphor as somehow adequate for grasping the hierarchical relationship between a monopolistic underground train service and the way non-running trains let down the stranded commuter – wouldn't it?

In his very useful book, *The Limits of Interpretation*, Peter Lomas writes of the parental metaphor in another way when he says, 'We can . . . very easily find ourselves, in spite of logic, regarding the major figures who control our lives – those with more power than most of us – as a kind of parent . . . In other words, it seems to be rather difficult for us to be in a situation in which we are cared for without it reminding us so much of our childhood that we find ourselves feeling like a child.'[10] He gives an example of his reaction to a road accident to note how 'in everyday life we are in situations – mild or extreme – in which the world relates to us in ways that have marked similarity to the condition of childhood'.[11] However, I have my own experience like this. When I was in my early twenties I crashed my motorbike and when I woke up on the road aware of a lot of blood in my mouth and with the ambulance crew examining me, I remember thinking 'Something really bad has happened here. There is nothing I can do. I am going to let them take over completely. I am entirely in their hands.' In other words I realised I was totally helpless due to my injuries and needed immediate care and attention. But I really cannot say I felt like a child, or that the ambulance crew felt parental from my own perspective, and I equally do not think that they regarded me as a child or themselves as parents in their caring role either. I certainly remember being totally helpless and in the hands of a greater power. Rather than parents, I was in the hands of fate or God as 'projected' – or fantasised – on to the paramedics and later the nurses, doctors and the whole hospital system.

Thus, there can be at least two readings of the parental metaphor. Freud pointed out how our beginnings as more or less helpless infants in the hands of a more or less powerful and more or less caring parent gets replayed not only in the transference relationship with the therapist, but even in our religious belief – where our relationship with God is no more than a replay of our earliest experience of the omnipotent father parent. Jung took a rather different perspective on this. Rather than making the parent-child relationship the primary source of all subsequent helpless/powerless-helpful/powerful relationships, Jung reversed the hierarchy. God is no longer a simple re-experience of the all-powerful father known in infancy, but the infant's father in fact offers the infant a re-experiencing of God in a religious, emotional and psychological sense. It is this we take with us through life. It certainly fits my own experience: when critically helpless as a young adult I was in God's hands.

Lomas compromises his own accident experience, however, with, 'I felt like a helpless child in the hands of Godlike parents'. In my view, the key words in his statement are 'Godlike' (as the omnipotent, all-powerful Other) and 'helpless', not 'parents' and 'child'. I think this because of these three points:

- Not all helplessness is childlike.
- Not all children are always helpless.
- Not all parents are helpful – or, indeed, powerful!

The therapist and analyst has been compared to the priest as much as to the parent.[12] And although a priest may be referred to as 'father' and a senior nun as a 'mother superior' – thus retaining the sense of a parental analogy – their key role is as representatives of God, or, rather, as interpreters or guides in the affairs of God and humanity. Indeed, a priest recently told me how the Church is distancing itself from the priest-as-father/mother analogy in an effort to emphasise a more shared role between priest and congregation. This role emphasises that human affairs and human being are not simply conscious, rational, logical and clearly visible to human beings, but include a greater vision which can only be glimpsed or worked at gradually and carefully. Thus, this role implies the potential for spirituality. Again you can make the comparison that the child's view of the world is similarly restricted and often discovered through the filter of, and helped or hindered by, the adult parent or teacher. But I believe there is a far more useful way of viewing all the images of the 'powerful' that we choose to represent – according to our own disposition – as God, priest, parent, doctor or therapist. The image that psychoanalysis and analytical psychology provide as the powerful Other to our helpless, powerless human conscious self is, of course, the image of the unconscious. The human psyche is subject to this powerful part of ourselves that may undermine or enhance our lives at any time, so it is no wonder that it has been conceived of for some – recently for Jung, but across aeons for humanity in general – as God or analogous to God. For Freudians of all sorts, on another scale but relative in terms of a power differential, it is conceptualised as the result of experiencing an all-powerful parental – meaning mother – environment earlier in life.

The archetype of the wounded healer

Another understanding of the relation of the unconscious to the conscious mind is the way it may be regarded as Other and thus a form of Nature – and subsequently not like a consciousness characterised as human. A Nature, moreover, within our psyche. Our conscious minds have an ability to understand, and to communicate, representations and images (emotional and cognitive) about humans and Nature, and the ability to invent ways of acting upon humans and Nature, which has first established and later enforced a distinction between the human part of the world and the rest that we call Nature. Consciousness recognises that Nature has many forms, some more similar to the human than others (dogs as opposed to trees for example). It also acknowledges that, 'logically', we humans must also be 'part of Nature', while holding fast to the distinction that humans must be classified also as *apart* from Nature. For a period, from the Enlightenment until the end of the nineteenth century, this separation became extreme and any sense of the Nature 'within' us was minimised as humans went about investigating and exploiting various other humans and non-human others of the natural world in the name of a new human activity called 'science'. But Freud and Jung's redis-covery of the unconscious mind restored the idea of Nature 'within' humans in a psychological form, where it took the place once occupied by the soul or spirit.

Jung, especially, had a particular way of conceiving the unconscious self – or the 'objective psyche' as he called it – emphasising it as the powerful Other within. While Jung's understanding of the personal unconscious was similar to Freud's unconscious and populated by the fallout from our biographical history and the 'family romance', it was also influenced and shaped by what Jung called the 'archetypes of the collective unconscious'. Archetypes are structuring principles in the psyche that are only known to us when consciously experienced as affects, images, thoughts and behaviours (including those images we consciously remem-ber from dreams and fantasies). Archetypes in this sense are entirely and typically human.[13] There is one such archetype that is worth close scrutiny when it comes to what goes on in psychotherapy between therapist and client, and one that is useful in unravelling issues of power in that context, probably a lot more useful than analogies with God, priests and parents. This is the archetype of the wounded healer.

All archetypes consist of opposing poles and tend to split unless we integrate their effect consciously. As the name suggests, there is a wounded (sickness) aspect and a healer (healthy) aspect to the archetype – a division, which produces problems, as we will see.[14]

Jung revised Freud's original psychoanalytic theories and techniques in a direction that went some way to challenging power differentials between analyst and patient that prevailed in the early years of psychoanalysis and still exist today. For one, he preferred a face-to-face setting for therapy, so that both the therapist and client can see the expression on each other's faces. This links with the way he viewed both participants as having part of their psyche always unconscious and how the therapist – although professionally paying attention to this – was not privileged in his or her relation to the unconscious. At a certain level, the therapist does not know any better than the client what is going on, and the task of therapy becomes a *mutual* exploration. Jung's perspective seems unique in the world of therapy. He maintained that in every analytic or therapeutic encounter, both the therapist and the client will be affected by, and will change in the course of, the work.

This sounds close to Winnicott's analogue of the therapeutic pair as mother and child and how both play and develop together in communication and knowledge (and it certainly fits with Daniel Stern's view of development). Lacan, too, acknowledges that both therapist and client are subject to the same repression that creates what he called the 'symbolic order' – the unconscious in a general cultural and linguistic sense. He, too, noted how the therapist is always regarded as 'the one supposed to know', and how one task of the therapist is to help the client see that this is not so and that they too can, if not 'know', at least achieve a relationship with the limits of 'knowing' which, as human beings, therapist and client alike have to accept.

Returning to Jung's emphases, he also maintains that any therapist cannot take the client along the path of insights, transformation and healing further than the therapist has been able to go in their own individuation or therapy. Ideas around the archetype of the wounded healer connect with this point inasmuch as everyone who trains and offers themselves as a healer of their fellow human beings in some respect needs to have an awareness of, and a particular relationship with, this archetype. Whether they be doctor, nurse, social worker or psychotherapist, they need this capacity for awareness not only in themselves, but in their fellow human beings in general so they may help others access this human capacity for self-healing. This does not make the particular expertise of the trained professional redundant, as one might think, but it certainly shifts the emphasis of what the task of healing is all about. Rather than it being a matter of offering expertise and skills only possessed by the therapist and not the client – including the psychotherapist's rather particular skill to spot their own images and emotions as generated by the patient's trans- ference and countertransference effects – the wounded healer implies a far more humble attitude to the work. Acceptance of this image and this aspect of our human being, not only by professionals but by all of us, puts a limit on what the ego – meaning our perception and will and the relation of these to 'reality' – can achieve when acting from one person to another. It shifts the perspective from a powerful position of expertise and responsibility invested solely in the healer or therapist, to one in which both healer and the 'one to be healed' are required to accept an Other that is the possession of both. The one to be healed needs helping towards trust in this psychological and emotional attitude; the healer, the therapist or the doctor, needs to trust this just as equally.

It seems, then, that the task is more a matter of overcoming distrust in the processes of the psyche, the unconscious, Nature or God however we call it, and setting aside grandiose assumptions about what rational intentions may achieve on their own. In effect, this attitude to healing is a reversal of Enlightenment assumptions about the power of the rational mind and a return to effective belief in what 'scientific rationality' has disregarded for the last five hundred years.

All this comes with a warning, however. The Jungian analyst Adolf Guggenbuhl-Craig has written about the two poles of the wounded healer in his book *Power in the Helping Professions*.[15] The two poles of the wounded healer archetype are conveyed in a more down to earth fashion as a *health-sickness archetype*. Trainee medical doctors often imagine they suffer from the illnesses they come across in their patients:

> Older doctors smile at their fear-ridden students . . . and ascribe no importance to it. But this so-called neurotic phase can be a turning point for the medical student . . . However, very often the burden is too great, and the pole of sickness is repressed. But if he is capable of experiencing sickness as an existential possibility in himself [or herself], and of integrating it, then the student becomes a true 'wounded healer'.[16]

Guggenbuhl-Craig goes on to point out how when more power is exercised in the medical profession 'the less the genuine healer appears'.[17] But he also emphasises that 'it is better for the doctor to try to reunite the split archetype through power than simply to ignore the split-off pole altogether'.[18] Guggenbuhl-Craig points out that the wounded healer is not one who sentimentally *identifies* with the patient but, 'The image of the wounded healer symbolizes an acute . . . awareness of sickness as the counter-point to the physician's health, a lasting and hurtful certainty of the degeneration of his [or her] own body and mind. This sort of experience makes of the doctor the patient's brother [or sister] rather than his master.'[19]

A parallel example of power and the split archetype is that of a mother in relation with her daughter: here, the mother needs to be aware of the daughter in herself lest she become 'only a mother', that is, trying to be a perfect mother without weaknesses:

> In such a case the daughter becomes a total daughter, helpless and completely reliant on the strong mother. The

mother rules her daughter with power. No 'motherliness' is constellated in the daughter herself; nothing maternal inside her begins to care for herself, and no daughter is constellated in the mother. The relationship is that between a strong, dominant mother and a weak, dependent daughter.[20]

And the key thing to note in this example is how the desire for power and the subjugation of the other – no matter how subtle or disguised or justified – is itself an attempt to heal the split archetype of mother-daughter in the person exerting power – just as it is in the case of the power differential between therapist and client, where it is a matter of health and sickness: the wounded and the healer. In every case, the problem arises from the split between the two poles, the non-integration of two opposing aspects of our humanity. These are aspects that belong together in all of us, but which become subject to powerful projections and maintenance of the splitting precisely because we are trying to heal them. This is why power has a point, but how in the end power will not achieve its aim. Therapists making patients the object of their power drive does not heal the split between health and sickness. But neither does renouncing their own power as this in itself is a self-empowering ploy, as Nietzsche and Foucault have pointed out.

So what does heal the split? Guggenbuhl-Craig notes that there are genuine 'wounded healers' out there:

> ... they are therapists in whom the archetype is not split. They are, so to speak, constantly analysed and enlightened by their patients. Such an analyst recognizes how the patient's difficulties constellate his [or her] own problems, and vice versa, and therefore works openly not only on the patient but on himself. He remains forever a patient as well as a healer.[21]

However, more often than not, the therapist tends more and more towards one side of the polarity the role of *only the healer* and 'hence the false prophet and the charlatan'.[22] Guggenbuhl-Craig recommends not more analysis, or even more supervision or discussion with colleagues, but more relationships with friends who are disconnected with the profession and with children – both of which will challenge the therapist's assumptions about their own self-knowledge, and replace smugness with a deeper awareness of power in relation to their patients. In just the same way, teachers, police, politicians and all of those engaged in human activities involving authority and hierarchy would do well to observe themselves in this way.

Conclusions

I am glad to have been able to offer a different parent-child analogy just now when I used Guggenbuhl-Craig's comparison between the mother-daughter split and the healer-wounded split. It really brings home how power differentials in our relationships are so active precisely when we seek to be most benign and helpful.

We have travelled some way in this chapter from Foucault's pointing out how power is subtle and absorbing and not merely forbidding or repressive. I considered how in-egalitarian relationships in our society – especially those between parents and children – have provided a model (and a mask perhaps) for the practice of psychotherapy which is just as much subject to unequal power relations as are most human relations in our culture.

I concluded with a consideration of Jung's emphasis on a different technique that starts by acknowledging that therapists and patients are joint and equal subjects in the work of psychotherapy (despite their apparently different positions and roles). In the example of psychotherapy, Guggenbuhl-Craig's consideration of the wounded healer shows how power tries to heal the split between health and sickness in all of us. We are all, whether patient or therapist or whatever, neither 'wounded' nor 'healer' but are both. It is not only the case that all therapists 'have been' both, but they are also not able to rest complacently behind some alternative, and equally powerful, mask of wounded healer as if their own need for healing were over. Like all other human beings, therapists were 'wounded and healer' then, are 'wounded and healer' now and are 'wounded and healer' from now on.

Each new day, each new person should remind us of both aspects in ourselves, just as therapists need to remind themselves of the healer and not just the wounded in their clients.[23]

Notes

1 Foucault, M. (1967) *Madness and Civilisation*, London: Tavistock, and (1974) *The Archaeology of Knowledge*, trans. A.M. Sheridan Smith. London: Tavistock.

2 Rabinow, P. ([1986] 1991) *The Foucault Reader*. Harmondsworth: Penguin, pp. 51–2.

3 This is more of the order of the problem in Joseph Heller's book *Catch 22* where a pilot seeks to leave combat service by pleading, or rather, claiming, insanity. The catch – and this is the original 'catch 22' we now coin when we refer to all sorts of double-binds – is that you would be insane to want to stay in the war of your own free will, therefore, if you want to leave you must be sane after all! In this case, the culture of combat has absorbed the 'defence' of insanity that would otherwise be valid in other terrible human situations outside the war. Power resides in that absorption of the discourse about what is sane and insane, and thereafter no repression of freedom is required. The pilot need not be forced to stay flying, it is the reversal of meaning of his own terms which keeps him there.

4 Rabinow, P. ([1986] 1991) *The Foucault Reader* Harmondsworth: Penguin, p. 61.

5 Ibid.

6 Ibid., p. 62. This point of view is even more valid when we consider the effects of widespread publicising of cases of child sexual abuse, with the result that parents, especially fathers, have become self-conscious and over-cautious in their attention to normal activities – like bathing, dressing and swimming – that involve contact with their children's bodies.

7 Frosh, S. (1987) *Psychoanalysis and Politics*. London: Routledge.

8 Perhaps Freud's analogy of horse and rider which he applied to the relationship between id and ego may return!

9 We will tend to notice this in other areas such as the weakening of

political hierarchies through the growth of single-issue lobby groups, and reverses in hierarchies that benefit consumers over producers.

10 Lomas, P. ([1987] 2001) *The Limits of Interpretation*. London: Constable, pp. 96–7.

11 Ibid., p. 98.

12 Ellenberger, H. ([1970] 1994) *The Discovery of the Unconscious: The History and Evolution of Dynamic Psychiatry*. London: Fontana.

13 Although at the far end of a continuum they encompass, they are rooted in instincts – whatever these are – and embedded in the matter of the body which itself is, ultimately, just matter. Hence their connection with the non-human Other of nature while being, as we know them, centrally human.

14 It is also interesting how aspects of the wounded healer may be seen to clash with other dominants in the contemporary psyche such as the culture of the expert – which may be understood as one side of another archetype the *senex* or wise old man. The other pole of this is the *puer* or *puella* – the eternal boy or girl who accompanies our wise maturity.

15 Guggenbuhl-Craig, A. *(1971] 1999) Power in the Helping Professions*. Woodstock, NY: Spring Publications.

16 Ibid., p. 90.

17 Ibid.

18 Ibid.

19 Ibid., p. 89.

20 Ibid., p. 88.

21 Ibid., p. 120.

22 Ibid.

23 Under such circumstances, our knowledge also lies with the patient's knowledge and thus our power lies with both of us as well. A patient arrived on a rainy day in cream trousers and jumper and I noticed she had splashes of watery mud all up the back of her trousers. I would not normally say anything but somehow felt I wanted to comment on it, and mentioned she had these muddy marks. She was surprised as she did not know this had happened. But then she sat down and immediately told me that today she was wearing 'all white' while her boss – who she finds rude, bullying and difficult – was wearing all black. At this I said, 'And he has splashed some of his black on you.' She went on to talk about how on two recent trips to Berlin with him, his behaviour had offended her – and the Berlin colleagues – and just the previous morning he had been criticising her in a phone call that brought her to tears once she had put the phone down. However, she had stood up for herself and not let him steamroller her and she said that later in the day 'he was nice to me' – but not apologetic. I congratulated her on her handling of this as before we had talked about how easily she flies off the handle with her boyfriend and in casual

encounters with others such as a cleaner at the office. Our conversation led to the way she had been seeing matters too much as 'black and white', right and wrong (with her in 'the right' of course!) rather than being able to discriminate and see shades of grey – meaning a range of possibilities rather than simply one thing or another. The aggressive behaviour of her boss towards her appeared very unfair but in this case, due to his powerful position, she could not simply attack back but had to take account of his character and appropriately manage to stick up for herself at that moment. What she was beginning to get to grips with was how different people and different contexts need a range of responses from her based on two perspectives that are new to her: first that she can be more flexible in her needs and values than she has been, and second that other people are all rather different and she needs to discriminate between them and approach them differently (also depending on context) rather than believing them to be (as she has believed herself to be) simply one thing or another. (And also surrendering her false ideals about how others should always behave.) Thus she is splashed with grey, things are muddier than she thought and my untypical comment – deriving more from a social exchange than a therapeutic one at first sight – turned out to be very much part of the therapy. This was something my unconscious 'knew' but I consciously did not know at the time. I benefited from trusting my impulse to speak up even though I had no idea it was relevant and in fact thought at the time, 'Why am I mentioning this? It's a bit out of the frame isn't it?' In the end I too was finding a flexibility in what I 'should or should not' say to the patient that moved us beyond my own black and white ideas of what is done in therapy.

Secrets, sex and being young

In his semi-autobiography written just before he died, Jung wrote, 'There is no better means of intensifying the treasured feeling of individuality than the possession of a secret which the individual is pledged to guard'.[1] He lists many experiences he had as a young man but he fails to mention sex, let alone masturbation. Sexual experiences are the first private, secret experiences a young person discovers. Up until then, the young person's life is lived in the context of, and under the gaze of, adults who care for them and protect them. Once sexual feelings appear and get expressed in a variety of experiences – alone or with a partner – these are realised as *private experience*. The youngster now has something that is entirely their own, something that makes him or her more 'me' than ever before. This is not stuff to be discussed with mum and dad in the car or at the dinner table like, 'How far away is the moon?' or 'Why do people starve in Africa?' or 'Mum, have you heard of David Bowie?' Sexual experience, especially when first encountered, is impressive in its intensity and in the way it has nothing to do with anyone else. Least of all the generation above.[2] When understanding adults allow it to be reserved for the young individual in this way it becomes highly confirming of the young person's sense of themselves. It forms a marker for their growing sense of individuality.

Perhaps that is why the Victorians and others frowned upon masturbation and extramarital sex so much. If the aim is a cohesive and hierarchical society, the last thing those in power wish to encourage is a sense of individuality that might challenge the order of things. Reservation of sexual experience solely for married citizens turns this most private of experiences into public property. In spite of its image as a private romantic event, marriage is a highly significant public ritual involving promises made in front of others – including promises referring to the body and sexuality, and the law. In a typically human effort to manage the nature in ourselves, what marriage does is to turn sexual experience into a matter of legitimate public concern. But when sex can be kept secret, when it need be of little concern to others because those involved are young and have no significant social function as yet, we should appreciate and honour the secret. Sex helps adolescents to feel who they are: individuals emerging from the parental matrix, being themselves and finding their own relationships to the rest of the human community.

Notes

1 Jung, C.G. (1963) *Memories, Dreams, Reflections*. London: Flamingo. The scholar Sonu Shamdasani has pointed out how this book is not written entirely by Jung himself. See Shamdasani, S. (1995) 'Memories, dreams, omissions', *Spring Journal of Archetype and Culture*, 57, pp. 115–37.
2 This is why the sexual abuse of young people by those of an older generation is particularly grave. But this is a much more complex matter that cannot be dealt with here. As for so-called 'sex education', all that is necessary are clear biological facts detailing health, hygiene and the physiology of sexual arousal and reproduction. All the other very important stuff – emotions, relationships, ethics and judgments of normality – should be taught, or will get learned anyway, alongside many broader aspects of life beyond the sexual. All this 'information' is far too complex and experience-dependent for us to expect adults like teachers or parents to cover it. It takes years to learn, so let's leave the first sexual experience – that of individuality – alone.

4

Ethics, difference and Disneyfication

> Through his identification with the collective psyche [the patient] will infallibly try to force the demands of his unconscious upon others, for identity with the collective psyche always brings with it a feeling of universal validity – 'godlikeness' – which completely ignores all differences in the personal psyche of his fellows.[1]

The reflections on power in the previous chapter call for a dicussion of ethics and difference, which are under consideration in this chapter. There is a tension between the two ideas of 'ethics' and 'difference' which I wish to exploit. The idea of ethics implies a standard of 'right' and 'wrong' – a morality or code that all agree to abide by. It implies similarity and lack of diversity; in fact a code of ethics is thought to be necessary to provide guidance and thus limit diversity in professional practice that could prove to be harmful. Diversity as perversity. An ethic not only provides a standard way of going about things – a way that also defines 'best' practice – but it also promotes itself as *the* standard – the position from which all other varieties of diverse belief and behaviour shall henceforth be judged. I will be writing mainly about psychotherapy but, as with the previous chapter, my points could apply to any number of professional services and activities where there is a risk of one human being exploiting another, when they are meant to be helping.

Difference could not be more different. Difference refers to the range that any phenomena may take – it draws our attention to the idea that, although we may prefer standards and starting points and essential values, these all exist relative to other comparable values. There are different ethics and different moralities. In fact, if these differences did not exist we would not need to be defining our own values and moralities as ethics. So, while these concepts are in tension with each other, they are also clearly dependent upon each other. They are also in danger of negating each other. Too much attention paid to difference and ethics might as well go out of the window. Too much value placed on the essentialism of one code of ethics and all difference is squashed – subsumed under a single, standard value. Once again we are back with the tension between the two.

In this chapter I will be recalling what was said earlier about opposites as an approach to understanding such things. I suggest that this tension between ethics and difference can be examined through an analogous opposition: that of the *individual* and the *collective*. Postmodern psychology – along with much postmodern thinking elsewhere – is keen to pay attention to the tension between these two, and Jungian psychology in particular is useful in this respect. This is because the Jungian concept of the unconscious psyche recognises both an individual and a collective element which exist in the same way as the personal and the social aspects of our being exist in the outer world of day-to-day life. But I will start by saying something about postmodern views on how, on the one hand, we differentiate and make difference through our use of language and, on the other, how we represent similarity and sameness through the images we use.

Difference and sameness

Difference has taken on a special character in postmodern epistemology. A particular focus within postmodernism has been language itself, with the emphasis on its limitations. The late French philosopher Jacques Derrida introduced the seriously playful idea of *différence* – from the French verb *différer* which not only means to 'differ' – to be unlike or dissimilar – but also to 'defer' – to postpone or delay.[2] Langauge is a system of signs – *signifiers* – that refer to phenomena and objects in the world. These referents – the things being referred *to* – are known as the *signified*. We rely on the idea that a signifier such as the sound pattern 'dog', for example, refers to a concept we all hold of a 'dog'. Instead of presenting what we are referring *to* – the actual corporeal 'dog' – we employ the sign or signifier 'dog'. In that way, Derrida maintains, by using the language sign, we mark an absent presence. Instead of presenting a dog we use the sign 'dog'. The reality of the actual dog, and hence the 'final' meaning of our utterance 'dog' is 'deferred'; the meaning is permanently postponed just at the moment when we think we are precisely defining that meaning.

Another way of considering this is Derrida's concept of *sous rature*, a term which is usually translated as 'under erasure'. This refers to the practice of writing a word and then crossing it out but keeping both the word and its deletion. This is intended to convey how the word – any word – is both inadequate (or inaccurate) and so must be crossed out, and is also indispensable, so must still remain legible. Because words are always defined by other words, as well as by the context or sentence in which they are placed, the final meaning of any word or collection of words is, again, permanently deferred because the same word may be found in another context and then another, endlessly.

Now imagine if a code of ethics was to be addressed by this deconstructive practice! By pursuing this line we would have to confront the idea that, while trying to construct and define our ethics using the tool of language we not only define the distinctiveness of a certain point of view, but also permanently defer any final meaning. At the moment of our most precise attempts at setting standards we are at our most vulnerable moment of putting off what we mean to say.

As soon as we define something we should or should not do – the making of an ethic about a 'right' or 'wrong' – we have to name it. I would like to evolve my argument on ethics using a particular example. The code of ethics devised and approved within one major psychodynamic psychotherapy training, a code that has been influential in guiding others' codes of ethics, involves a clear statement that there should be no touching between therapist and client. From what I have said about *différence* and under erasure we can see how the postmodern critique of language may also apply to the language of ethics in psychotherapy. In this example, we are seeking to say something about 'touch'. But the meaning of 'touch' varies across different people and different circumstances. To take an extreme comparison, think of the arm of a mother around her child's shoulder and then think of the arm around the same child's shoulder but this time belonging to a convicted paedophile. Your perspective immediately changes; the touch is the 'same' but each touch is also radically different.

Moreover, in my example, the ethics statement when referring to touch does carry the caveat that despite the 'no touching' standard, it is understood that under some circumstances the client may 'need to be restrained'. In other words, the only 'touch' that is 'right' is the prohibitive touch, the touch that stops or prevents or restrains an individual.

These guidelines – like much of what goes on in the profession of psychotherapy and analysis – are influenced by standards stemming from the medical profession. But when it comes to doctors and touch, what makes one touch ethical and another not? This question is especially pertinent when it comes to touching sexual parts of the body, as in gynaecology and genito-urinary treatment and examination. What makes the difference between the touch that is 'right' and the touch that is 'wrong'? Is it purely the *intention* of the doctor? How can this be proved or disproved as unethical?

What about the problematic idea of gratification – which presumes the touch must be in the service of healing and not for the gratification of the doctor's desire. Doctors develop their specialisms in connection with the gratification that their work gives them. Psychotherapists are presumably gratified by the intimacy with another that their work offers. If this is the case, what type of gratification would be unethical – and how could you tell?

Any consideration of difference – different touches or whatever – bears a relationship to sameness and similarities. Ethical standards are meant to be adhered to in a similar fashion by all those who agree to them. By having such agreed standards, the practice governed by them is assumed to be conducted in a similar fashion wherever it is encountered. But what is the fantasy that has guided the forming of these ethical standards – which is what we call the similarities – in the first place?

This makes me think that some of these ethics and standardisations are tending to take the form of what another postmodern theorist, Jean Baudrillard, refers to as the *simulacrum*.[3] Just as we live in a culture governed by language we are also influenced by a vast range of representations. The human psyche seeks to represent the world to itself not only in language but in a vast range of images, both individual and collective. We like to think that these representations are useful simulations that represent something that exists elsewhere, but in postmodern culture there is a tendency to generate representations of something that has never in fact existed. This is what is called the simulacrum: it convinces us it is a representation, but what it represents has never in fact existed. My own favourite example is the purpose-built street in Manchester that the public may visit as if they are actually walking on the 'real' Coronation Street, past the houses of people known to the visitors. The fact that the people are characters played by actors, and the 'street' is a film set built with all the materiality of any northern England street, does not seem to detract from the 'authenticity' of the experience. In this case the Coronation Street television set is a representation of a reality that does not exist outside the pages of a television script, the imagination of the art department and the fantasy of its viewers. For all its appearance of 'reality' there exists no other reality that it represents: it is a simulacra.

In the case of psychotherapy, its image of itself, its values and to some extent its ethics, I think the fantasy is of that room in Berggasse 19, Vienna, with a couch draped with Eastern rugs, a patient lying supine and, at the head and at right angles to the patient a bearded Moravian man puffing on a cigar. There is a good deal of psychotherapy today that persists as a simulacrum of Freud's original conditions and method – a representation of something that never existed in the pure form that the fantasy suggests.

For instance, it has occurred to me that the much-practised silence of the psychotherapist derives less from ideas of a 'blank screen' psychoanalyst than it does from those followers of Freud influenced at the time by how he was growing more and more silent. But Freud's apparent withholding of comments arose less from theoretical – or ethical – reasons than due to the fact that from about 1923 his cancer and his poorly-fitting oral prosthesis was making it harder and harder for the poor man to speak. On the contrary, he had a great deal to say to patients in the early days, and subsequently, as his writing indicates.

Many of the ethical positions taken in psychotherapy are structured around this Berggasse 19 fantasy and they then form a standard that all therapy is meant to observe in quite a strict fashion. What we would end up with – if psychotherapy completely followed this standard – would be a sort of stereotype: a cartoon image or, perhaps worse, a Hollywood image of psychotherapy. Baudrillard refers to Disneyland as a prime example of the simulacrum, but Hollywood films, and soaps like *Eastenders* and *Coronation Street* are good examples too. I think we should question the extent to which we are Disneyfying psychotherapy at the very moment at which we want to make it more serious and reliable as a profession. Other human practices like the police may have also begun to suffer from the effects of their *fictionalised* TV counterparts on the one hand, and the equally

Disneyfying attempts to portray their activities in 'fly-on-the-wall' documentaries on the other. Ironically, these films which position themselves as presenting factual material in contrast to fictional versions, merely construct a further set of representations, a further fantasy that is even more insidious. It is even called 'reality TV' while it is nothing of the sort but simply more simulacra.

To summarise what I have said so far: in the example of psychotherapy, ethics form part of the effort to standardise working practices so that across a wide range of treatments of individual clients by individual therapists, there will be a similarity of boundaries of behaviour and of expectation of what goes on. Such a sameness is in tension with an equally present and necessary difference between individuals and between the styles and approaches of individual therapists. Language – the very stuff of a defined code of ethics – conveys meaning by denoting what differs from what; it differentiates meaning. There is also the postmodern point of view that points out how language also *defers* meaning – in other words, differentiating meaning through language is forever postponing any definite meaning. The presence of meaning in a word signifies an absence at the same time.

My other point was this: the structuring of ethics in psychotherapy seems to be the concretisation of a fantasy of what psychotherapy *is* – what it aims to achieve and the conditions and method necessary to that aim. In these legislative days we have been required to make a representation of psychotherapy partly structured around the standardisation of ethics. I have been suggesting that this representation or simulation is a simulacrum that only 'represents' itself. It is a Disneyfication of psychotherapy based on nothing that has existed apart from a fantasy based on the image of Freud's 'original' method.

I realise these are powerful criticisms and I now wish to corral these issues around ethics, difference and the simulacrum within a framework of thinking derived from Jung's psychology. This is the psychology of the individual and the collective and the differentiating from collective psychology that Jung calls the task of individuation. Moreover, indi-viduation – the task of becoming an individual, which lies at the core of any therapeutic aim – holds, for Jung, a specific moral imperative. In this view, a version of a human being human, the differentiation of the individual is also the ethical development of the individual. Here, difference and ethics coincide.

Individuation and the collective

Jung's view of our psychology holds that, in addition to the ego – the centre of consciousness, which is a concept shared with other psychologies – there is an unconscious which has two 'levels' to its structure. Unlike psychoanalysis, Jung posits a personal unconscious and a collective unconscious. The collective is distinguished by how its contents have not been derived from personal biography as have the contents of the personal unconscious. Jung goes on to assert how human brains are uniformly differentiated as far as the collective unconscious goes: 'The universal similarity of human brains leads to the universal possibility of a uniform mental functioning'.[4] However, less well known is the way that Jung goes on to differentiate between two aspects of the collective unconscious itself. The collective unconscious not only consists of what he calls the universal collective psyche but also a collective psyche 'limited to race, tribe and family'. The former is our ancient phylogenetic inheritance built up over millennia of human existence, while the latter is an equally objective – i.e. impersonal – unconscious but one more closely related to the individual's personal unconscious and consciousness and its present environment. It is this collective unconscious, the one that causes individuals to identify themselves unthinkingly to national causes or collective movements, that Jung seeks to address when he refers to the 'morality of individuation', as I will discuss later. Jung makes his perspective quite specific: 'Our personal psyche bears the same relationship to the collective psyche as the individual to society'.[5] In the inner world as in the outer world, we are both individual and social creatures: 'And just as certain social functions . . . are opposed to the interests of single individuals, so the human psyche exhibits certain functions or tendencies which, on account of their collective nature, are opposed to individual needs'.[6]

Psychoanalytic views agree that raising the contents of the *personal* unconscious to consciousness is helpful to the healing and development of personality in psychotherapy, but it is quite another matter when it comes to the *collective* unconscious – in both its universal aspect as well as the more 'local' collective aspect. The assimilation of the collective unconscious can lead to dangerous inflations with psychotic and megalomaniac effects on the conscious personality. The individual personality is overwhelmed and distorted beyond a scale it can manage. This arises because, as Jung puts it:

The specific virtues and vices of humanity are contained in the collective psyche like anything else. One man arrogates collective virtue to himself as his personal merit, another takes collective vice as his personal guilt. Both are illusory as the megalomania and the inferiority, because the imaginary virtues and the imaginary wicked-nesses are simply the *moral pair of opposites contained in the collective psyche*, which have become perceptible or have been rendered conscious artificially.[7]

What psychotherapy might be able to achieve – a reduction in the tendency towards projections and symptom formation, through the integration of unconscious contents for the benefit of a more integrated personality – brings with it a risk of identification with the collective unconscious. Such an identification has the reverse effect on the individual personality: if the social collective values are believed in as 'my own', individuality has once again been compromised – just at the moment when it believes itself to be enlightened. Individual responsibility – and therefore individual ethical choice – gets clouded by collective material and values. The assimilation of the collective – in the same way as an undifferentiated assimilation of society's values – runs the seductive risk of relieving us of our individual moral responsibility.

How can this be avoided while still retaining the benefits of integrating unconscious contents? The answer returns us to one of our key words: difference. It is the differentiating power of the human psyche that is the vital element here, 'since', as Jung puts it, 'partial or blurred differentiation leads to an immediate melting away of the individual in the collective'.[8] Without a strict differentiation of personal from collective unconscious contents, the individual runs the risk of imposing a moral assuredness upon others with all the certainty and universal validity the collective unconscious tends to carry for the individual under its sway. This is the 'godlikeness' that Jung refers to which 'completely ignores all differences in the personal psyche of his fellows'.[9]

Interestingly, Jung also emphasises that, apart from the suffocation of the individual, this also results in 'a ruthless disregard . . . of differences of a more general kind within the collective psyche itself, as for example differences of race'.[10] I discuss this theme at length in Chapter seven but for now I will simply point out how this is one of those instances where Jung, far from being racist as he is often accused, is at his most contemporary in pointing out and celebrating the importance of what he calls racial difference but which we would understand now as *cultural* difference.

Size matters – but what makes a difference?

Moral and ethical choice always lies with the individual and the freedom necessary for such choice. Jung claims that there is an inverse relationship between the size of a society and the morality of that society, and that this is because individual factors, especially morality, get blotted out. Jung puts it this way: 'The larger a community is, and the more the sum total of collective factors peculiar to every large community rests on conservative prejudices detrimental to individuality, the more will the individual be morally and spiritually crushed, and, as a result, the one source of moral and spiritual progress for society is choked up.'[11]

Such a restriction of the individual arises from the way in which all the collective qualities in a community's individual representatives results in putting 'a premium on mediocrity, on everything that settles down to vegetate in an easy, irresponsible way'.[12] The process starts in school and continues into higher education and then continues in large businesses, the state apparatus and professional institutions. In small bodies there is a greater chance of retaining individual freedom and moral choice, but with state legislation now imminent for psychotherapy in the UK it too has become a mass community within the greater mass of society. What chance is there for retaining the moral freedom of the individual, which is so vital for living an authentic life?

The key to this issue is something mentioned earlier: the differentiation of the personality – not only the differentiation of unconscious from conscious contents but the further differentiation of the personal unconscious from the collective. This process of differentiation Jung called *individuation*. Individuation is the urge found in all living things to persist in becoming themselves; in human terms this means the development of the individual personality and becoming the person you were meant to be or the person you have always had the potential of being. Jungian psychotherapy has this as its central aim and objective. It lies at the core what I mean by *human being human*.

But, critics ask, why does this individuation not lead to *individualism* – a sort of self-centred concern which ignores the wishes and needs of others – the very inverse of an ethical stance as we might understand it? In a nutshell, Jung's answer is this: 'Since the individual is not only a single entity, but also, by his very existence, presupposes a collective relationship, the process of individuation does not lead to isolation, but to an intense and more universal collective solidarity'.[13] This is because the individual *per se* is the vital lynchpin, 'determined on the one hand by the principle

65

of uniqueness and distinctiveness, and on the other by the society to which he belongs'.[14]

There can be no 'morality of one'; a code of ethics implies a collectively agreed standard which also acts to override individual moralities, preferences or beliefs. If a practitioner wishes to touch a client (on the hand or shoulder, for example) the ethics of the organisation says they should not be doing so. In our part of the world – the northern European collective – there is a general aversion to touching except in circumstances where the context involves intimacy in all its varieties. Elsewhere in the world, touch between people in many circumstances – formal greetings, family contact, child and adult and so on – is far more the norm. Here I am thinking of the kiss on the cheeks between male friends, for example, in Mediterranean and mid-European countries, which is avoided in favour of the handshake in British and North American society. Avoidance of touch under some circumstances might not only be viewed as rude but as also indicating a degree of pathology in the touch-averse individual.

A key aim in creating ethical standards for psychotherapy is the protection of clients (and, consequently, therapists too) from the risk of any abuse of the therapist-client relationship. If we then find that, for some, complete abstinence from touch is an abuse for that individual, we are back in the frame of individual rather than collective beliefs. Or, more accurately, we are in a different frame of collective beliefs and values, which are now manifest through this unique individual who is different from us. Perhaps this is a theme that might guide us: if a collective ethic overrides the individuality of a certain client or a certain situation, then that ethic should be assessed for its application or not in that individual case. By having ethical standards, we are far from being in a position to abandon individual differences as and when they occur. And if this is true for the individual therapist with his or her individual clients, how much more so is it true for the range of different therapies and psychologies treating different individuals in a variety of different ways?

What is required is an obstacle-free, two-way street between individual values and collective ethics. This does not mean the abandoning of all standards as if anything goes; but it does mean ongoing hard work that examines and re-examines what therapists, and other professionals, believe they are doing in the practice of their professions. On the one side, none of them should rest on a platform of ethical standards drawn up in their name as if this will always be correct and reliable at all times. Neither, of course, should they be going about their practices in an individualistic way as if the rest of the world and the profession were of no consequence. But by developing their individuality along the lines indicated by Jung's concept of individuation they could be in a position to simultaneously develop not only their own personal creativity but the moral and ethical strength of an entire community.

Deferring the last word

To finish, I would like to recall what I was saying at the beginning about language and difference and how the word also defers any final meaning – how language puts off meaning at the very moment we think we are using it to have the 'last say'. This theme connects with the problem of Disneyfication I have also mentioned.

One part of our postmodern scene is the tendency towards a universalising of culture, images and beliefs – a universalising led by the West and especially the USA. Believe it or not, I heard the other day that the image of Mickey Mouse is the most universally recognisable in the whole world. (Yes, more than Jesus or Buddha and certainly more than Freud or Jung or The Beatles, Bush or Blair. Though the Coca-Cola logo probably comes a close second.)

With the need for legislating within large, even global, communities, comes the belief that universal standards are both desirable and possible. Although this might be a very good idea in the case of, for example, the engineering profession and their attention to something like the manufacture of steel girders so that bridges all over the world can be relied upon to stay up, I have my doubts about whether this is desirable or possible for human activities like psychotherapy treatment, where individual differences are crucially present in the work. When it comes to people, as Jung emphasises, 'Suppression of individuality through the predominance of collective ideals and organisations is a moral defeat for society'.[15]

The last thing we want is a Mickey Mouse code of ethics, implying a universal template that results in the trivial and insubstantial. Equally, a shared code of ethics – no matter how desirable – is not going to let us off the hook as if such a collective effort can release us from still having to make our own individual choices time and time again.

The attitude illustrated by Derrida above points out how our confidence in the language that we use tends to mask how we are at the same time postponing the meaning that we meant. A reflexive attitude – something psychotherapists should be good at – is critical in all this. All such professions would benefit from developing an ongoing conversation between the individual and the collective – not only in the outer world of people and society, but also in the internal struggle between what is individual and collective in their own personal experience of being human.

Notes

1 Jung, C.G. (1928) *The Collected Works*, Vol. 7. London: Routledge & Kegan Paul, para. 240.
2 Derrida, J. (1978) *Writing and Difference*, trans. A. Bass. London: Routledge & Kegan Paul.
3 Baudrillard, J. (1981) *Simulacres et Simulation*. Paris: Galilee.
4 Jung, C.G. ([1953] 1977) *The Collected Works*, Vol. 7, *Two Essays on Analytical Psychology* London: Routledge & Kegan Paul, para. 235.
5 Ibid., para. 234.
6 Ibid., para. 235.
7 Ibid., para. 237, italics added.
8 Ibid., para. 240.
9 Ibid.
10 Ibid.

11 Ibid.
12 Ibid.
13 Ibid., fn. p. 155.
14 Ibid., para. 519.
15 Ibid.

'I lived with the speaking clock'

Long before I even thought of training as a Jungian analyst, I lived with the speaking clock. He was not the speaking clock at the time, of course. That happened afterwards. I shared a flat with him in Brighton, in the South of England during 1982 and Brian Cobby – that was his name – worked as a telephone operator for the national telephone company. I was working as a van driver delivering paper bags to grocery shops all over the county. Adams Paper Bags was run from a medium-sized, end-of-terrace Victorian house, with a shop area downstairs, some offices above, and a yard for the van and storage of bags at the back. It was a small family business run by Mr Adams, his wife, his daughter and his daughter's husband. There was another young man who went to get the orders for the bags and then there was me who loaded the van with Mr Adams' help and drove off to deliver the goods. I was taught a lot about bags and wrapping paper, I earned £57 a week and I saw a lot of the greengrocery business.

But all good things come to an end. I had the offer of a place at the University of London to study psychology and anthropology, and as soon as I was given a support grant I decided to leave Adams Paper Bags and take up the place. Mr Adams was upset when I announced my decision late that August. 'You teach someone the business,' he said, 'then they just up and leave.'

I went to live in London and did well in my degree. I began a Jungian analysis in my second year, got a social work job and eventually began training as an analyst with the Society of Analytical Psychology. Meanwhile, back in Brighton, my old flatmate Brian had entered a competition for the new recording of the telephone speaking clock and he had won! He was the first male voice they had used and I think he was paid £5000. You can hear him anytime you dial 123 in the UK. Because of the novelty of his voice, not to mention his ebullient personality, I saw him on the television several times after that. So we both did well. My life changed radically after I left Adams Paper Bags. That year in Brighton had been another world and I never thought about the place again until

I met a colleague who trained as an analyst in the same institution as me but a little after.

I knew he lived in Brighton and I asked him how he and his wife found working down there – availability of clients, type of cases and so on. He said they did not work at home but they had bought premises which they had converted into rooms for themselves and for other therapists. When he described the house and where it was it turns out he had bought Adams Paper Bags. Adams Paper Bags – where I had arrived every day at eight o'clock to load my bags – was now a clinic for the psychotherapists and their clients. It seems Mr Adams had had enough, he retired and my colleague bought the place. That job driving a van for Adams Paper Bags had seemed the nadir of my life and, since then, it had stood as the complete opposite of my subsequent interests and achievements. It is astonishing how both our fates – mine and that of Adams Paper Bags – curved back to meet each other. As someone once said, *les extrèmes se touchent*. Or, once you head far enough away from where you began, you start approaching again from behind.

And another thing. People still don't believe me when I tell them I lived with the speaking clock.

5

That thinking feeling

Psychotherapy and the fear of the intellectual

The psychologist and writer James Hillman once gave a talk entitled: 'Getting in touch with your thinkings'! This strikes us as funny because it surprises us with a reversal of what we expect to hear. Apart from treatments that are explicitly 'cognitive', just about all other forms of psychotherapy pay greater value and interest to the emotions and affects, and 'getting in touch' with these. At the same time, the intellect and rational thinking tend to be demonised as the mental activities, which can lead us astray and distort our 'authentic' 'feelings' about things.

This, of course, is a complete reversal of – and a challenge to – the dominant cultural emphasis on rational thinking. The latter, as we saw, has stemmed from the European Enlightenment which established the view that it was the human intellect that was the pinnacle of what made us the superior species, while the emotions were to be discouraged and disregarded as misleading, primitive, childish and altogether too close to the animal. The emotional was an interruption of the rational and thus had to be managed for human scientific and intellectual progress to forge ahead.

Depth psychology, with its emphasis on the irrationality of the unconscious, was a reaction to the Enlightenment's emphasis on the intellect and consciousness alone. It took further historical and cultural factors to push this reversal towards a bias, which favours the emotions and criticises the intellectual. I will go into these factors shortly.

Given that this bias exists, perhaps the question psychotherapy should be asking is: 'What is wrong with the intellectual?' This may need to be followed up with, 'What is wrong with rationalising and what is wrong with thinking, that we should be so critical of these in psychotherapy?'

I think the answer would come back a number of ways, which are pretty easy to detect from the literature of depth psychology in general. For one thing, intellectualising in therapy is seen as a defensive or resistant strategy on the part of the client. In responding to the therapist or to their own material in an intellectual fashion, the client is regarded as avoiding the emergence of unconscious contents that may be uncomfortable and challenging to consciousness and self-identity. The client may also be intellectualising as a way of avoiding emotional reactions and impulses that are similarly undesirable to consciousness.

Intellectualising, otherwise known as abstract thinking, is not the same as thinking *per se* and neither is it the same as rationalising. It can be best described as logically scrutinising material – one's own behaviour or personal circumstances for example – in a detached, objective fashion which excludes emotion like an idealised form of science. Rationalising is also regarded as defensive and resistant of the therapeutic process; it is a way of 'making sense' of material that comes up along the lines of rational norms either derived from society at large or from more personal perspectives. Like intellectualising, therapists regard rationalising as a way of refusing or pushing away material emerging from the unconscious or assimilating it rapidly – and incompletely – so that the uncomfortable challenge to the conscious ego is minimised.

So far, these answers square with a classical psychoanalytic view that the psyche seeks equilibrium – pleasure even – and will avoid discomfort. But the rejected, uncomfortable material retains its pressure and if not integrated with consciousness will manifest itself in symptoms. Therefore, the story goes, it follows that intellectualising and rationalising are to be discouraged and challenged by the psychotherapist so that the unconscious may be known and integrated with consciousness, no doubt leading to the relief of symptoms and a degree of change in the conscious attitude.

So far, so good. Let's keep the intellect and its trickster techniques branded and corralled. Let it dare toss its head and the therapist will rope it in – all in the name of making the unconscious conscious, and in the name of 'getting in touch with how you feel about this'. Like Freud's image of the ego mastering the id like a rider controls his horse, the rodeo analogy gets extended from the reining in of our instincts to reining in our intellectual resistances.

From the Jungian point of view there is some support for this approach – but the emphasis here is less on the defensiveness and resistance of the intellect and much more along the lines of a cultural and historical critique. Jung emphasised how contemporary consciousness had evolved in a lop-sided fashion so that ego-consciousness over the last six hundred years had grown to regard itself as the central, if not the sole, aspect of what is was to be human. Similarly to what I have written about intellectualising, Jung writes:

> modern man's consciousness has strayed rather too far from the fact of the unconscious . . . the intellect has no objection to 'analysing' the unconscious as a passive object; on the contrary such an activity would coincide with our rational expectations. But to let the unconscious go its own way and to experience it as a reality is something that exceeds the courage and capacity of the average European.[1]

For us to really encounter the unconscious in Jung's view, it is necessary to de-emphasise the intellect, which has become the dominant mode of consciousness. His phrase was *abaissement de niveau mentale*, a lowering of the threshold of consciousness to allow space for unconscious contents to emerge, and for ego-consciousness to know these contents and be affected by them. The aim is to allow the irrational contents of the unconscious to be restored as valid aspects of the psyche as a whole.

But is this process identical to one in which intellectual, rational thinking approaches are suspended so that affect and emotions may powerfully emerge? Maybe yes, and maybe no. On the one hand, unconscious contents may well be accompanied by powerful emotions, whether these are stemming from the personal unconscious and individual biography or from the collective unconscious, and reveal wider aspects of our humanity. On the other hand, unconscious material may have a weak emotional content. It may consist of imagery that informs and amplifies consciousness but is far from overwhelming in an emotional sense. It is still material from the unconscious but it may not have the grand emotional valency – 'numinosity' for some Jungians – psychotherapy tends to value. It may even be the case that, for some therapists, low emotional valency leads to a distrust of, and a lower regard for, such imagery as somehow less authentic and therefore less important to what therapy should 'really' be about. We will deal with the possibility that the unconscious may have its own rationality presently.

At this point it should be mentioned how that same old Enlightenment that privileged rational thinking achieved this by fooling us into believing that intellect and affect were opposed in the first place. I have written about this in a chapter of *Jung and the Postmodern*, but the crux is how – as the European psyche evolved to achieve the style and degree of discriminating consciousness we experience today – affect had to be opposed to intellect in the same way that 'man' was necessarily opposed to 'nature'. The seventeenth-century proto-scientist Jeremy Bentham said of the scientific application of human rationality that we should 'put Nature to the rack to force her to yield up her secrets'. The affects would have ambivalently clouded such ruthlessness. Emotions were regarded as an interruption to man exercising his awesome power to intellectually chop up the world into portions of knowledge by which that same world might be manipulated and exploited. What we have forgotten is that this was simply a ploy: there is no actual division of intellect and affect, there is no actual split between thinking and emotion. Consciousness was fooled and then, four hundred years later, along comes psychotherapy and says we have to put the whole thing back together. What I point out in my chapter 'Affect and modernity'[2] is that Jung's concept of the archetype – the unconscious structuring of our inner and outer realities – explicitly makes no such division. Archetypes and their manifestations have aspects that are cognitive, intellectual, aesthetic and emotional all at the same time. It is this aspect of psychotherapy that tends to heal the intellect-emotion split much more than the pointless reversal involved in the dismissal of intellect in favour of 'getting in touch with' the affects.

Nevertheless, intellect and a certain type of thinking do have to make way, according to Jung, to allow the unconscious to become available to consciousness and thus to overcome the split. But for Jung, unlike so much psychotherapy since, the split is not between thinking and feeling – by which I mean the experiencing of affects – but between two kinds of thinking: intellectual directed thinking and undirected fantasy thinking. When it comes to his psychology, Jung's emphasis is clear when we note how he devotes one line to a definition of 'intellect' and six pages to a definition of 'fantasy'! Of 'intellect' he simply says: 'I call *directed thinking* intellect'.[3] Moreover, in defining what he means by these various 'thinkings' Jung states, 'Active thinking is an act of the *will*, passive thinking is a mere occurrence . . . Active thinking, accordingly, would correspond to my concept of *directed thinking*.'[4]

Jung says he used to describe passive thinking as 'fantasy thinking' but things actually get even more complicated. In his list of definitions he now calls 'passive thinking' *intuitive thinking*.[5] And he defines the difference thus, 'The capacity for directed thinking I call *intellect*; the capacity for passive or undirected thinking I call *intellectual intuition*'.[6] Thus, by bringing together two terms from either side of the active/passive thinking divide, it appears that the polar-isation of fantasy/intellect is far from hard and fast: in this formulation, undirected, passive, intuitive thinking is also 'intellectual' – and valued as such.

Moreover, when it comes to the third aspect of intellect/thinking/rationality, Jung asserts that directed thinking is rational because it arranges ideas according to a rational norm of which we are consciously aware. By contrast, undi-rected thinking is irrational because it arranges ideas in a way that is not consciously observed as rational and there-fore cannot be recognised as being in accord with reason. However, the outcome of undirected, passive or fantasy thinking may still be rational even if it came about in a way that appears irrational. What this amounts to saying is that there are irrational paths to achieving rational outcomes. Rational thinking is certainly not the only route to a rational conclusion. Intuitive leaps and dream imagery are famed for their power to produce great science. This works the other way too: rational thinking can lead to outcomes that appear irrational as when powerful intellects work on the phenomena of particle physics and achieve conclusions that are, for many, worryingly irrational according to the norms of classical science and so-called 'common sense'.

But the 'emotional' side of the coin is not exactly simple either. Modern usage often substitutes the word 'feeling' for the experiencing of emotions, but Jung's particular use of 'feeling' makes it rather different from the idea of 'emotion'. For him, the feeling function does not refer to 'emotional' (although, as I am emphasising, there is emotion attached to every function), but to an evaluative, judging function of consciousness. Of this he remarks: 'Thinking that is governed by *feeling* I do not regard as intuitive thinking, but as a thinking dependent on feeling . . . in such thinking the laws of logic are only ostensibly present; in reality they are sus-pended in favour of the aims of feeling'.[7] In other words, there is a type of thinking that is subsumed beneath, not emotion, but the pressures of judging and evaluating which may not accord with what is rational.

So, how far have we got in our assessment of the roles and merits of these aspects of psyche: intellect, thinking, rationality, emotions, fantasy, intuition? They are clearly all useful approaches to perceiving and experiencing ourselves and the world. For much of psychotherapy, emotions are valued over activities of the intellect, thinking and rationalising. For Jung, fantasy is promoted in favour of intellect. But we have also seen how everything, including emotions, fantasy and intuition may be regarded as 'rational' – a position which overcomes the Enlightenment accusation of the irrationality of anything but the intellect. We have also seen now how the intellect – although rational – may lead to apparently non-rational conclusions. This requires us to conclude – along with Jung and many a social anthropologist since – that there is more than one kind of rationality.[8]

Thinking: the post-war years

At this point I need to mention a second historical and cultural factor that has contributed to the skew away from the intellect and towards the emotional in psychotherapy. This is the inter-wars shift – especially in British psycho-analysis – away from a father-dominated depth psychology to one in which the mother and her nurturing qualities tends to contour what psychotherapy is all about. It was summed up in Janet Sayers' title *Mothering Psychoanalysis*.[9] Whatever we may think of the emotionally nurturing qualities of mothers or fathers, within a patriarchal culture like ours these matters tend to get split so that human qualities become regarded as the property of one gender or the other. Hence the post-war object relations, attachment theory and Kleinian views, which focused on early infancy and the bond with the mother, resulted in a further downplaying of the intellect and thinking – infants not being regarded as strong in these areas – and a dramatic reification of the importance of emotional bonds. The shift for psychoanalysis was the binding together of instinctual and emotional drives – as played out in the mother-infant scene – and this rapidly became the focus of the aim of psychotherapy. More women joined the profession than ever before once the cultural bias toward a link between females and emotional nurturance found a new basis in psychodynamic theory. No matter how true or invalid the association of women, nurturance of infants and emotional literacy may be, out of these social-historical circumstances psychotherapy became weighted further towards the emotional side of its material.

From its late nineteenth-century emergence as a reaction to Enlightenment bias toward the intellect and rationality, depth psychology reduced its original focus on the irrationality of the unconscious – in its multitude of manifestations – to concentrate, more or less entirely, on its emotional aspect alone.

This historical aspect to the fear of the intellectual, and the involvement of gender, has further implications. In the novel *Pilgrim* by Timothy Findley we witness a fascinating reconstruction of the lives of Carl and Emma Jung and goings-on at the Burgholzi hospital in the Spring of 1912. In one scene, Emma is in bed and Carl starts getting excited about a new idea he is developing:

> 'Emma please. Just stay awake long enough to hear one last thing.'
> 'Yes, Carl Gustav. But tell it quickly.'
> Jung sat forward. He had – but why? – an erection.
> [His inner voice speaks] You get too excited Carl Gustav. You get too excited about ideas.
> I can't – I can't help it . . . I hadn't thought I wanted to – but there it is. Jesus. Look at it.
> [His inner voice replies] I don't need to look at it. I can feel it. What you suffer from – amongst other things – is nothing less than intellectual priapism. It's that simple. Get an idea – get an erection.[10]

There *is* something phallic and arousing about the intellectual approach: it makes its presence felt in a thrusting, creative fashion. But in doing so, emotion is not necessarily excluded or avoided at all – there is great passion in intel-lectual ideas. And despite how Jung, himself, quite wrongly wrote off 'women's thinking', neither is the 'feminine' eclipsed by the intellectual: women, of course, have pas-sionate intellectual approaches as well. However, Jung is also attributed with the phrase: 'The penis, too, is a phallic object' and, just as feminism restored confidence in the feminine intellect, feminist writers point out that women also have their share of erectile tissue. The intellect is neither the property of the phallic male nor is it divorced from powerful affects.

Concluding emotions or a thoughtful ending

I would like to start bringing these views together now around this chapter's topic – that thinking feeling and psychotherapy's fear of the intellectual. Whatever you think, having a mind is a complex business. All the time we are thinking, feeling, intuiting, fantasising and emoting with little conscious distinction between these functions. It is when we are being dragged in opposite directions by these psychic activities that we get distressed, or get into trouble with our relationships and maybe seek help from a therapist. At this stage, the last thing we need is to be told off about our 'thinkings' and encouraged to become more 'in touch with our emotions'! Many people who come to understand themselves and their relationships better do not achieve this in a one-sided fashion led purely by their emotions or their fantasies: this would be as useless as purely *thinking* themselves out of their tangles. Our psychological activities and experiences progress in a more pluralistic fashion where no single mode dominates for long but all aspects interact and, ultimately, work in cooperation. There is a Buddhist psychological approach I have found helpful: they advise dealing with affects in an affectual way and dealing with intellectual thoughts in an intellectual way. That is, valuing the mode that is dominant from time to time and letting the action of that mode itself inform the psyche as a whole. This is an educative approach whereby thoughts, fantasies, feeling values and emotions are learned about and clarified within the mode in which they are appearing.

What I think goes wrong in our efforts, sometimes (in psychotherapy and in general), is the way in which we get lost in an ongoing *translating*: the translating of emotions into thoughts, of feelings into intellect, of fantasies into meanings or of intuitive knowledge into affect. Psychotherapy is too strong on translation – it has a clever name for it: *interpretation* – but it still involves taking the language of the client and overlaying it with the language of the therapy (whether this language stems from the therapist, or from the cultural discourse of therapy that clients themselves employ in their self-translations).

However, I do not want to bring all these psychic elements together and fudge them all in some fantasy of wholeness. But, just as we are no longer Enlightenment rationalists like Bentham or Locke, neither are we nineteenth-century modernists determined in our opposite reaction to their position. I am recommending a different attitude: one that places intellect, thinking, fantasy, intuition and affect on an equal footing. Each has their place in our pluralistic and multi-dimensional psychic life. True, some of these psychic functions will be found to be resistant to unconscious contents from time to time – but it really is hard to tell which one is the main culprit. Emotional modes can be as resistant as intellectual ones; on their own, some types of fantasy can get you nowhere in terms of the unconscious; and unexamined intuitions can certainly lead you up the garden path.

By privileging emotion over intellect, or fantasy over other thinking, we are promoting a psychotherapy that is as anachronistic and uncomfortable as a penny farthing bicycle where the huge drive wheel dominates a far smaller wheel used only for the steering. This image also says something about the relationship between an academic approach to the psychology of the unconscious and the corresponding 'clinical' practice of psychotherapy. Making such a big wheel out of the clinical scene distorts the project as a whole and runs the risk of us all falling off into the road. Maybe clinical therapy fears the intellectual in a similar way to which Enlightenment rationality feared the emotional. Powerful positions are often maintained on the principle of 'divide and rule' – especially when legitimated by claims of expertise on the psychology of 'splitting' itself! Could it be that the clinic is wary of the academy because it poses a threat to therapeutic thoughtlessness, undeclared and denied power needs and fundamentalist complacency? When it comes to psychotherapy and the fear of the intellectual, or how we live our psychological lives as human beings in an everyday sense, in addition to developing a pluralistic attitude maybe one way forward is to feel that fear and do it with feeling anyway.

Notes

1 Jung, C.G. (c. 1953) *The Collected Works*, Vol. 12, *Psychology and Alchemy*. London: Routledge & Kegan Paul, para. 60.
2 Hauke, C. (2000) *Jung and the Postmodern: The Interpretation of Realities*. London: Brunner-Routledge, pp. 223–35.
3 Jung, C.G. (1971) *The Collected Works*, Vol. 6, *Psychological Types*. London: Routledge & Kegan Paul, para. 766.
4 Ibid., para. 830.
5 Ibid.
6 Ibid., para. 832.
7 Ibid., para. 833.
8 See for example, B.R.Wilson (ed.) ([1970] 1981) *Rationality*. Oxford: Basil Blackwell.
9 Sayers, J. (1991) *Mothering Psychoanalysis: Helene Deutsch, Karen Horney, Anna Freud and Melanie Klein*. London: Hamish Hamilton.
10 Findley, T. (2000) *Pilgrim*. London: Faber & Faber, pp. 257–8.

What's wrong with 'Hollywood' anyway?
Making money and meaning

I have found images derived from movies tend to speak volumes for the contemporary understanding of ourselves as human beings. Our visions of the current state of humanity are both led by and enhanced by the photographic image, which can be as informing as it can be distorting. Either way it provides a tool by which we define ourselves and by which we can become defined.

For the USA and the rest of the world, the film of the second aeroplane hitting the Twin Towers on a sunny September day in New York in 2001 is as iconic as the footage shot by Mr Zapruder in Dallas in 1963 is of its own time and place. In 1969 I saw two 'Hollywood' films (as we have come to call them) in different cinemas in one afternoon. In those pre-multiplex days you had to walk across town to achieve this. One was *Midnight Cowboy* from which I retain two scenes – Dustin Hoffman crossing the Manhattan traffic as Rizzo, hitting the car bonnet and shouting, 'I'm walking here' and, later in the film, dressed in his Hawaiian shirt and dying of pneumonia on the bus to Florida. The other film was *Easy Rider* and the scenes of Hopper and Fonda crushing a wrist-watch in the dust, riding their motorcycles across the Huey Long Bridge to Jimi Hendrix's 'If Six Were Nine', only to die shot by rednecks from a pick-up truck. I was 16 and these movies helped define my attitude to the world at that time. Since then, great films (and other film images derived from news and documentaries) have formed a time map of my life and my emotional engagement with and understanding of the world. They have not been the only contributor of course, but they have been very important to me and, I reckon, millions like me.[1]

Before films were ever invented, human beings collectively projected the unconscious psyche onto stories, myths and folk tales handed down from generation to generation in oral tradition. As consciousness evolved, differentiating exponentially over the last 600 years, the unconscious has contained more and more of our collective human potential that is ignored and devalued in the present era. The dominant consciousness of modernity eclipses an Other

83

Figure 5.1 Easy Rider (Columbia / The Kobal Collection)

comprising the feminine, the mytho-poetic, the religious, mystical, spiritual, subjective and uncanny while promoting the fantasy of a detached, objective rationality as the dominant world view. In our postmodern times, this type of consciousness has invented technology such as photography, moving pictures (and now digital media) which have, ironically, given us a technique of projection that is capable of reflecting back to us what we once lost. Nowadays, and on a massive collective and cultural scale, psyche is returned to us through projection of the celluloid 'moving' image on the cinema screen. Cinema has become the place where we gather together in the dark to witness the story and participate emotionally in sharing the projection.

Given the huge influence of the moving image – and given some people's concerns about its power to create views that can become closed to debate – rather than dismissing movies why not get to grips with understanding their significance for our human being at this time?

Close your eyes for a moment and think of a special place, one that is set apart from daily life, and one where you go and sit for a period of time which has a beginning and an ending planned beforehand. You go to this place anticipating a greater involvement with and experience of your own emotional reactions together with those of other people in a transpersonal and collective human fashion. It sounds like a church doesn't it? It also sounds like a group psychotherapy session. But what I am thinking of is the experience of the cinema. Watching a film at the cinema involves a similar containment to what Jung called a *temenos*. This is a Greek word for the sacred precinct around a temple where the presence of the god may be felt. It is not the holy centre itself – that might be the personal inner experience – but neither is it the street where ordinary life goes on. The cinema is a special place, set apart from daily life and always in darkness, where we stay for a period bracketed by the time it takes to screen the film. And, like a church, this is all done collectively, in the company of others. Here, all our eyes are trained in the same direction. This is not a regular social occasion, so, as in psychotherapy, ordinary day-to-day talk is not exchanged.

And, while everyone is aware of sharing the same experience, it is also the case that there are as many individual varieties of that experience as there are seats in the cinema.

Cinema as a *temenos* offers the possibility of movies becoming an imaginal space where we may engage with the unconscious just as we do when we pay conscious attention to our dream images and other fantasies. In addition to this, and similar to a Jungian psychotherapy session, the experience of film offers a special place where psyche can come alive, be experienced and be commented upon with some detachment as if observed from the outside. Popular cultural forms such as cinema can provide the safe place that is necessary for intense experiences, making them more accessible and more bearable. This brings with it the possibility for psychological and emotional repair and growth. As in therapy, the raw material offered by cinema is made available in a form that the psyche can work upon more consciously. Jung noticed that 'The cinema, like the detective story, enables us to experience without danger to ourselves all the excitements, passions, and fantasies which have to be repressed in a humanistic age.'[2] What I think he means by 'a humanistic age' is that, in our times, we do not go to the Colosseum to watch gladiators, but we watch *Gladiator* as a Hollywood spectacle and no one really gets hurt.

We live in times where we still pay poor attention to our unconscious processes, our images and dreams. But contemporary culture offers compensatory opportunities. The cinema film has become the medium that is able to direct all of us back towards the unconscious psyche in this postmodern era. Postmodern attitudes value subjective experience and small-scale collectives; cinema involves individual experience side by side with shared experience. So, it is no drawback that the majority of films are produced for mass consumption. Cinema represents a rebirth of a collective, shared experience not unlike religious ritual in former times but one which, nowadays, places great value on the subjective view of each individual observer as well.[3] Steven Spielberg, whose films have been central to the revival of popular cinema since TV threatened to empty the cinemas after 1950, seems to understand this. Although he operates within the commercial pressures of an industry driven by the need to ensure mass popular support of its projects, he says, 'that's a blessing in disguise because it will bring us back to the story and the characters. It will compel us to return to the source of all great story-telling – the human soul and how it suffers and celebrates. *Let's go back to finding out who we are – not necessarily what we are capable of constructing*'.[4]

Notes

1 A friend of mine, Madelon Sprengnether, Professor of Literature at the University of Minnesota, has written a marvellous account of the way in which a dozen films have pinpointed key emotional phases in her life in her book, *Crying at the Movies (A Film Memoir)* published in 2002 by Graywolf Press (St Paul, MN).
2 Jung, C.G. (1931) 'The spiritual problem of modern man', in *Collected Works*, Vol. 10, *Civilisation in Transition*. London: Routledge & Kegan Paul, para. 195.
3 You only have to consider the care with which major feature films are previewed in front of non-specialist audiences whose opinions are sought and recorded meticulously. The views of these people are valued as much as those of the director, writer, editor, cinematographer and actors who have laboured over the film for years. Although the aim of the studio is to maximise popularity, this is clearly more than some cynical marketing effort. The way that creative film-makers respect the preview process suggests they know films only work when they touch upon collective needs and collective interests. Without this, movies would not only fail to make money, they would fail to make *meaning*.
4 Taylor, P.M. (1999) *Steven Spielberg: The Man, His Movies and their Meaning*. London: B.T. Batsford, p. 72, italics added. Luke Hockley's *Cinematic Projections the Analytical Psychology of C.G. Jung and Film Theory* (2001) University of Luton Press, Luton, expands on several ideas I have mentioned.

6

Is modern consciousness different? Modern consciousness and the quest for spirituality

The first question: perception and consciousness

We have just been examining the relationship between thinking and emotion and how we prioritise or integrate these and other functions of consciousness. In doing so, it has been necessary to refer to a historical perspective ranging from Enlightenment perspectives on human consciousness through to nineteenth-century revisions with the reintroduction of the concept of the unconscious, and twentieth-century developments that restored the role of emotions in our conscious life. This chapter pushes this line of thinking further by asking, 'Is the consciousness of modern human beings different from that in other eras – specifically that of the pre-modern, medieval mind?' The answer straight away must be 'Yes, of course it is.' But we should be clear about what we mean by this word 'consciousness'. We are not talking about *perception*. Perception is what happens when sense organs encounter a stimulus and register this in the neurological system of the organism. Consciousness itself differs from perception in at least two important ways. Firstly, consciousness always involves the *organisation* of perceptual phenomena. This includes both the *selection* of which aspects of perception are to be retained or discarded, and the *construction* of the element of consciousness that is finally arrived at. This is how, for instance, two people can perceive the same

Figure 6.1 Optical Illusion Old Lady/Young Girl

picture but have a radically different *conscious experience* of the picture.

We can have the same experience within our own conscious mind. Look at the picture on this page (Figure 6.1). If you focus in one place it looks like an old woman with a big nose; move your gaze and it looks like a young girl turning her head away. The perceptual object has not changed at all, but your *consciousness* of it – what this piece of the environment *becomes* within your psyche – has changed rather radically don't you think?

Secondly, consciousness, as cognitive science has established, is always trying to achieve a *completeness* of the sense perceptions it is receiving. The human mind is constantly trying to 'make sense' of the endless stream of perceptions pouring in through the sense organs. In other words, consciousness differs from perception because consciousness is always seeking to find, or construct *meaning*.

The Navigator: a movie

There is a film directed by Vincent Ward called *The Navigator, A Medieval Odyssey*[1] which I urge you to rent or buy so you may view it before or after you have read this chapter. The movie depicts a group of medieval folk in a mining village

in Cumbria, Northern England, in 1348. Under the inspiration of a 12-year-old boy visionary, Griffin (the eponymous
navigator), a group of men from the village undertake a
journey to complete a ritual act that has been foreseen by
the boy. Their village is under threat of the bubonic plague,
which has ravaged fellow humans in the distant city and is
now spreading to neighbouring villages. To save the whole
population the men have to undertake a sacred journey
culminating in the smelting of the copper ore they carry,
casting it into a Christian cross and finally climbing the
spire of a cathedral to place it aloft. They begin by boring
into the bowels of the earth, and in doing so, dig down into
the medieval past to emerge in the contemporary present
– stunningly evoked by their arrival beside a six-lane
highway busy with cars and trucks. This magico-realistic
odyssey culminates in the completion of their task and the
erection of the cross, over a single night in the terrifying,
huge modern city where their journey has taken them. It is
a journey from the past to the present, and from disease
to healing guided by the goal of a ritual act. The brutal
juxtaposition of the medieval and the modern in the film
stimulated me to consider what is different about modern
consciousness and to consider, in particular, what has
happened to our human need for ritual and for symbols. It
also made me think again about issues that originally brought
me to psychology, anthropology and Jungian psychotherapy.
These are issues around consciousness and 'rationality' – not
only the variety of 'truths' and world views available to the
human psyche, but also the danger inherent in a modern
narrowness of vision largely geared to material, practical and
financial purposes alone.

The second question: the construction of meaning

Our next question is this: what influences the constructions
of meaning and thus the differences in consciousness
between one group of humans and another? Briefly, there
are a number of social-historical differences between 1348

Figure 6.2 The Navigator (Arenafilm/John Maynard Productions/The Kobal Collection)

and the present day that we may wish to pay attention to. I make no attempt to be comprehensive here but will merely pick out some of the factors that come to mind.[2] On one hand, there is the dominant religious world view of this era: a degree of pre-Christian 'pagan' belief, but mainly influenced by the established Christian Church; Christian concepts of soul, sin and, above all, salvation – the reality of heaven and hell – constructed the universe and structured the conscious reality within which people lived. The vast majority of people were illiterate and relied on those who could read to bring them the 'Word' and interpretations that followed from religious texts. We can imagine how a human consciousness uninterrupted by the abstracting, structuring and informing power of the written word would tend to pay fuller attention to the immediate and concrete information derived from the senses. The immediate visual and spatial needs of the human body would predominate and, in this pre-machine age, would be enhanced by attention to the human body as the main instrument of labour.

However, in addition to this, as Richard Tarnas reminds us in *The Passion of the Western Mind*,[3] the thirteenth and fourteenth centuries saw an increasing interest in lay mysticism and a decline in the power of the established Church hierarchy:

> Intensely devotional, Christ-centred, and aimed at achieving a direct inner union with the divine, this religious outpouring took place largely without regard to the established structures of the Church . . . with such an emphasis on internal communion with God . . . the Church itself was seen as less mandatory for the spiritual enterprise. With advanced religious experiences now perceived as directly available to lay people . . . the priest and bishop were no longer regarded as necessary mediators of spiritual activity.[4]

Thus, as we see in the film, the time is ripe for the young, mystic navigator, Griffin, to lead his group on their ritual journey, thus depicting a consciousness not only Christian in its beliefs, but also 'pagan' and shamanistic in its actions.

Furthermore, European civilisation had started to enter a 'double-truth universe'. This state of consciousness became formulated in the philosophy of William of Ockham, which I will discuss presently. From the early fourteenth century there existed in European consciousness parallel paths of religious truth and scientific truth. It is this division that enables the navigators of 1348 to harness all their mining technology and knowledge for the purpose of their religious goal. They combine an active, practical contemplation – a worship of God with the whole of the body, specific application of mind and a fullness of the soul.

The beliefs of the Other: assessing different consciousnesses

Considering and assessing the differences in consciousness we come across is of central importance not only for these historical investigations, but also when we come to consider the 'otherness' of other cultural and ethnic groups and, in the field of mental health, the 'differences' we use to define the 'otherness' of psychopathology and madness.

Anthropology has long struggled with this topic, as Alisdair McIntyre describes in his essay 'Is understanding religion compatible with believing?'[5] He points out how the anthropological attitude to the 'beliefs of primitives' has moved on from Levy-Bruhl's[6] assertion that the thinking of natives is not mere ignorance but should be understood as 'pre-logical thought' – a view that influenced the psychology of Jung. Current views on the 'rationality' of others' beliefs address our own standard of rationality itself: 'Intelligibility takes many forms . . . there is no norm for intelligibility in general'.[7] Science and religion are modes each with their own criteria of intelligibility: 'Within science or religion actions can be logical or illogical.'[8]

However, such criteria – for science or for religion – have a history, and, McIntyre argues, when we come across a belief that challenges our own, instead of looking for what is special and present we should ask the alternative question: '*What criteria are absent from consciousness* to make this belief possible?' Can we understand only what fits into our own framework of understanding? What can we learn from societies that do not fit? Instead of checking off differences, why do we not take the opportunity to revise our own framework? The anthropologist Edmund Leach, for example, says that *statements* about *nat* spirits in the religion of the Kachin people in Burma are not statements at all and hence cannot be regarded as 'irrational'. Leach regards them instead as 'ritual performances which can be performed properly or improperly, but which are scarcely true or false'.[9]

When it comes to assessing different styles of consciousness, if we cannot avoid imposing our own criteria of truth we should at least do it reflexively and ask ourselves how 'they' would regard 'ours'. *The Navigator* depicts a version of this reflexivity in presenting a narrative which allows two belief systems to meet each other and leaves you, the viewer, to comment and decide. I have noticed how Australian and New Zealand film-makers often bring an awareness of still recent colonial encounters between European and native people in the South Pacific as we find in Nicolas Roeg's *Walkabout* and Jane Campion's *The Piano. The Navigator* retains the quality of this meeting of different conscious-nesses with medieval and modern world-views replacing those of the Aboriginal and the colonist.

Many thinkers such as Jung, William James and Carl Otto have pondered about what happens to the religious instinct for humans in industrial societies governed by scientific rationality. The internal contradictions of medieval belief – such as God's goodness and yet the existence of evil; or the coexistence of divine providence alongside human freedom – were nothing more than sustainable difficulties in conscious conception for the medieval world. Nowadays, modern rationality generally finds these to be final and sufficient grounds for religious scepticism and the abandonment of Christianity. As McIntyre points out:

> The apparent incoherence of Christian concepts was taken to be tolerable (and treated as apparent and not real) because the concepts were part of a set of concepts which were indispensable to the forms of description used in social and intellectual life. It is the secularization of our forms of description, constituting part of the secularization of our life, that has left the contradictions high and dry.[10]

'Protestant Christianity was itself a powerful secularizing agent, destroying in the name of God any attempt to deify nature, and so helping to rid the world of magic and making nature available for scientific enquiry.'[11] To grasp medieval Christian belief, McIntyre concludes, we have to 'supply a social context which is now lacking and abstract one which is now present . . . What is at stake is the character of difference between belief and unbelief as well as the issue of belief itself'.[12]

Cognition and the medieval mind

But how *do* we know *what* we know? How do we even *know we know* at all? The model of mind intuited by Descartes and Locke has proved unsatisfactory, and simply does not accord with contemporary cognitive science and other areas of knowledge. In an eloquent critique, Mikko Yrjonsuuri in his essay 'How did mental representation take place before the Cartesian theatre was opened?'[13] makes comparisons between the medieval thought of the type we encounter in *The Navigator* and the more recent concepts that were introduced via Descartes and Locke 300 years ago. He is inspired to do so by the criticisms of 'Cartesian theatre' Daniel Dennett provides in his book *Consciousness Explained*. This position views the mind rather like a stage upon which our thoughts are presenting themselves in a regular sequence. Locke discusses how the sensations of the sense organs reach 'their audience in the brain' – 'the mind's presence room'[14] as he calls it. These 'objects of thought' he calls 'ideas'. This perspective also entails a unified subject, the 'knower', implied by the idea of the 'mind's stage' (where there has to be someone sitting in the stalls, so to speak). And although this is the popular modern cultural image of our minds Europeans tend to live with, both these assumptions have been rejected by cognitive science.[15]

Dennett points out that while for Locke, red and blue seem different because they are different 'ideas' in the mind, cognitive science tells us different:

> For Dennett . . . red and blue seem different because their overall effects on our system of vision take different paths. No particular step in the experience can be called an idea, and there is no one thing (after the retina) in the two experiences that could be compared and found to be different. Vision of colour is to be explained by its multiple effects on our mind, not through representation by an object of thought.[16]

Dennett further denies the unity of the Cartesian theatre as developed by Locke when he points out there is no single mental subject collecting all thought or experience together in a single stream of consciousness as the old model implies.

It can be seen how the medieval view of mind offers us a contrast which suggests quite a difference in consciousness 400 years before Locke (1632–1704). For example, Thomas Aquinas (1225–74) explained the way a material object, like a table, could appear in the mind through the idea of *universals*. The table consists 'of a real universal and some designate individuating matter . . . When I see the table, the matter is left out by abstraction and the universal can be brought into the mind'.[17] It was William of Ockham (1280–c.1348) who developed this perspective. Ockham's own earlier work did retain universals, which sound very much like the Jungian concept of archetypes – 'the mind would produce universals, which would not really exist, but would be objects of thought within the mind'.[18] It is a short step from this to 'internal representations', Descartes and modern object relations. Duns Scotus (1265–1308) ushered in the more modern idea that an object can also have its own 'thisness' and the mature thought of Ockham razors away all universals – he becomes an extreme nominalist regarding all the so-called 'universals' as singular, as written or spoken *words*. Moreover he did not require any mediating or 'object of thought' in the mind but regarded the process as immediate and direct and called it 'intuitive cognition'.

The second step of the Cartesian/Locke view is the issue of *reflexive self-consciousness*: 'knowing' and 'knowing that we know'. Descartes defined mental activity in terms of consciousness alone: 'By the term 'thought', I understand everything we are aware of as happening within us in so far as we have awareness of it'[19] – in other words everything happening before the mind's eye on the Cartesian stage. Hence, it made no sense to suggest that there could be *unconscious thoughts*; Locke asserted it was 'nonsense to teach that the mind thinks even when asleep and unconscious'.[20] Thus we might reflect that the revolutionary challenge to

Descartes began in the late nineteenth century with ideas of the unconscious as conceived by Freud, Jung and their lesser-known precursors. Even so, Cartesian notions of the primacy of the mind as consciousness alone persist powerfully throughout modern culture. Descartes claimed that thoughts have an *awareness of themselves* and, in addition, that we also apply *reflective knowledge* to some thoughts. Previous to this, the medieval Thomas Aquinas denied any idea of such immediate awareness. For him, 'one's knowledge of one's own cognitive acts . . . [is] . . . based on second-order cognitive acts having the first-order as objects'.[21] Aquinas' view of our reflective cognition implies an infinite regression but, a little later, Ockham denies this by saying we are not aware of our mental acts – only God has that infinity of knowledge. Ockham also makes far less of a distinction between the external and the internal spheres of conscious-ness: 'In Ockham's approach, awareness of a mental act is similar to awareness of an external object'.[22] This is what ushers in the double-truth universe of both scientific and religious truth. In accordance with Christian revelation, Ockham viewed the mind as immaterial but he also, con-tradictorily, viewed the mind as an element of the natural world just like we, today, view the brain! Implicit in his thinking is a closer alignment of psyche and matter.

For Ockham the individuality of the human soul is not self-evident but is proved to be so 'because everything is . . . individual as an Aristotelian primary substance'.[23] In strict contrast to this view, Descartes, 300 years later, main-tained the soul is *individual* because it is experienced as *the subject of conscious experience*: 'I think, therefore I am' is Descartes' statement of the 'direct experiential certainty of his own existence'.[24] The Cartesian revolution was to prove 'the immaterial and immortal character of the [conscious] mind', but if we follow modern cognitive scientists in counter-revolutionising some of the Cartesian intuitions we 'may get to a stage where it is no [longer] strange to view matter as thinking' in a way that has been lost since the late medieval period.[25]

It is significant that this is exactly the direction of Jung's mature thought within his consideration of the psychoid, the archetypes and alchemy. Jung felt that the loss of the power of religious symbols and ritual in our Christian culture left a void that became filled by psychological symptoms – 'the gods have become diseases'. And this applied not only to individuals but, through the powerful projection of unconscious elements, led to whole nations becoming gripped by ideologies such as national socialism or communism in the twentieth century. Whether Jung is truly radical in his critique of modern consciousness and culture or, in his apparent return to a medieval and Christian faith in the value of symbols, he ends up as an irrelevant romantic and mystic, is a point we might wish to debate. Certainly his views on mind and matter and how these coincide with modern quantum science would seem to validate his position in line with the contemporary critique of mechanistic Newtonian science. His psychological views directly address the 'basic fault' in modern consciousness – the mind/body (and hence mind/matter) split based on the Cartesian model – which has resulted in modern mankind's experience of *lack* and the contemporary search for soul.[26]

These ideas will be followed up in the next chapter but, to come back to our film example, I would like to draw attention to the relationship between mind, body and the material environment in the activities of the medieval men and women in *The Navigator*. They are in an age of a rudimentary technology which is still very much an extension of human bodies. There is no power, like steam power for example, to supplement their own muscle. In the medieval era more power means more people working collectively. There is no alienation from their technology – with no steam engine there can be no individual ownership of its power, for example; the villagers' technology, reliant upon their bodies, remains within their own power. When they encounter the twentieth century they arrive with a sublime ignorance of the machine's blind disregard for human life that, in the late industrial era, erupted upon the consciousness of human beings. The closest version of this they had known was the power of nature or of God brought together in the plague disease, which they attributed to both. The medieval mind had no suspicion of what would later be the experience for the Victorians: the alienation from ourselves that machine technology accomplished.

In the film, the heroes emerge from the underground beside a busy highway and make attempts to cross; they are conscious of a danger but their experience limits them to perceiving the hurtling cars and trucks like they would a tricky fast-flowing river. When Connor, Griffin's heroic brother, attempts to outrun a diesel train we share his experience as a vision from hell.

It is for reasons of the body that the group undertake their quest and their task. The village is under threat of plague. Their journey, given in a vision to the young navigator, takes them from deep beneath the earth to the heights of a spire in the sky. Their task, to cast and then place a copper cross on the spire, takes them from earth, to fire, to water, to the air. Mind and body, psyche and soma are symbolically reunited with the elements of matter. The village is healed not so much by God's grace as by a conscious, effortful, involvement in matter. Artful activity and immediate involvement is all. When the medieval villager asks the modern foundry-man about casting his cross in the smelted copper his only question is, 'Can you do it? Can you do it?'

Notes

1 *The Navigator, A Medieval Odyssey* (1988) dir. Vincent Ward.
2 For a fuller picture I recommend further reading such as Edelglass, S. *et al.* (1970) *Matter and Mind: Imaginative Participation in Science*, Edinburgh: Floris; Wilson, B.R. (1970) *Rationality*, Oxford: Basil Blackwell; and the excellent *Understanding Consciousness*, by Max Velmans (2000, London: Routledge).
3 Tarnas, R. (1991) *The Passion of the Western Mind*. London: Pimlico.
4 Ibid., pp. 197–8.
5 McIntyre, A. (1970) 'Is understanding religion compatible with believing', in Wilson, B.R. (ed.) *Rationality*. Oxford: Basil Blackwell.

6 Levy-Bruhl, L. (1935) *La Mythologie Primitive*. Paris.
7 McIntyre, op. cit., pp. 65–6.
8 Ibid., p. 66.
9 Ibid., p. 69.
10 Ibid., p. 74.
11 Ibid., p. 75.
12 Ibid., p. 76, italics added.
13 Yrjonsuuri, M. (1995) 'How did mental representation take place before the Cartesian Theatre was opened?' in Pylkkanen, P. and Pylkko, P. (eds) *New Directions in Cognitive Science: Proceedings of the International Symposium, 4–9 August 1995, Lapland, Finland*. Helsinki: Finish Artificial Intelligence Society.
14 Ibid., p. 149.
15 Dennett, D.C. (1991) *Consciousness Explained*. London: Penguin. John Locke wrote in 'An essay concerning human understanding' (II, 8, 8), 'Whatsoever the mind perceives in itself, or is the immediate object of perception, thought, or understanding, that I call *idea*'.
16 Yrjonsuuri, op. cit.
17 Ibid., p. 150.
18 Ibid., p. 152.
19 Descartes quoted in Yrjonsuuri, ibid., p. 152.
20 Yrjonsuuri, ibid., p. 153.
21 Ibid., p. 154.
22 Ibid.
23 Ibid., p. 156.
24 Ibid.
25 Ibid.
26 See Tacey, D. (2001) *Jung and the New Age*. Hove: Brunner-Routledge.

'Nature must not win the game'

Under the ground and stretching along the walls in the subway station between 42nd St. and Sixth Avenue in Manhattan, New York City, there is an installation filled with words and images from sources as varied as Ovid, Joyce, nursery rhymes and Jung. Samm Kunce, the artist who made the piece says the words 'are ambiguous, I thought that's something that would keep the work alive'.[1] The whole piece is called *Under Bryant Park* in reference to what's on the surface directly above, and the quotation from Jung reads: *Nature must not win the game, but she cannot lose.* Samm says that her choice of Jung's words 'has to do with human imperative: our trying to control human nature – by, for instance, gardening – is an externalisation of the need to control our inner nature'.

There are big questions here, some of which get approached in this present book you are holding. I think Ms Kunce is on to something in her example of gardening but maybe not in the way she suggests. Gardening, the cultivation of nature, is far from being an activity unique to humans. Many creatures, such as leaf-cutting ants and bees who farm flowers for pollen to make honey, exploit their own environment to create something coherent and useful out of the opportunities offered by what are, otherwise, 'random' bits of 'nature'. Is any of this activity an externalisation of *their* need to control their inner nature? I don't think so.

What about the human cultivation of crops such as wheat and corn? Human beings do this to feed themselves more securely and efficiently rather than relying on gathering plants. It is the same story with rearing cattle, chickens and sheep for their meat, thus minimising the risk and effort of hunting and the possibility of coming home empty-handed. These activities are less about human beings overcoming the 'nature in themselves' and more about organisms sustaining their lives and producing a reliable food supply through their technical intelligence. I think you will find that it is not the *activities* that manage and control nature that refer back to inner nature, but the collective practices, rituals, fantasies and cosmological beliefs that arise out of them. We use our actual 'inner nature' – the instinctual pressure of hunger and our human desire to sustain our lives – as a force in itself. Our human being cannot be reduced to psychology any more than it may be reduced to biology.

However, since the Enlightenment promoted pragmatic, scientific rationality over many other resources which are as available and as 'natural' to our human lives, our exploitation of the world reveals a widening gap between human need and human need for meaning. Cultivation of the earth as an aesthetic rather than a food-production activity – in other words, gardening – is not merely the management of our nature in projection, any more than the culling of trees in Brazil or the harvesting of the North Sea fish is not merely a greedy conversion of a free 'natural resource' into hard currency.

Only in New York at the start of the twentieth century could an artist writing on a subway wall make the mistake of abbreviating the full quotation from Jung. Here, in one of the greatest of our communal, human, urban environments, yet one that has been created at great cost to both the human and the non-human environment, let us avoid the convenience of abbreviation and confront the rest of Jung's statement:

> Nature *must not* win the game, but she *cannot* lose. And whenever the conscious mind clings to hard and fast concepts and gets caught in its own rules and regulations – as is unavoidable and is of the essence of civilized consciousness – nature pops up with her inescapable demands. Nature is not matter only, she is also spirit.[2]

Notes

1 Samm Kunce interviewed by Andy Newman, 2004, 'Subway mosaic turns riders into underground philosophers', *New York Times*, 27 December.
2 Jung, C.G. ([1942] 1981) 'Paracelsus as a spiritual phenomenon' in *Collected Works*, Vol. 13, *Alchemical Studies*. London: Routledge & Kegan Paul, para. 229. For once, the italics are not mine but are Jung's own interesting emphasis in the original text.

Figure 6.3 Ground Zero, New York City

7

Racism, incest and the split mind of modernity: everyone is now a stranger among strangers

The price of hating other human beings is loving oneself less[1]

I wanted to place this chapter on racism after talking about the mind matter split because I believe racism represents another split between the sense of self or 'I-ness' and the Other. As I will show in the discussion which follows, racism not only reveals splits between individual human beings and our collective being as members of society, but it is also a reflection of the division within psyche itself .

Racism is always an individual, emotionally driven experience affected by a person's ability to deal with their own hostility, aggression and tolerance of difference. But it is also a social phenomenon that has powerful political, economic and cultural effects. It has a history in European nations and various forms of racism have contributed, and continue to contribute materially, to the type of civilisation we enjoy now and the political and economic shape of the world as we know it. Racism is an individual experience shaped in the context of collective social-political experience. More than this, like gender, it is informed by the collective and structured by the collective at an unconscious level. As Franz Fanon bluntly put it in 1967, 'The myth of the bad nigger is part of the collective unconscious'.[2] And as Paul Gordon writes, 'Racism is in the material world as well as the psyche and our attempt to understand it . . . must be in two places at once'.[3] A way of imagining these 'two places' might be to see each, the social and the psychological, as filters for the other. Social racism is filtered through specific psychological phenomena to produce individual behaviour in the form of an Enoch Powell, a violent BNP activist or a paternalistic slave-owner in the 1830s. Equally, changing social structures, economic needs and political values are filtered through individual psychology to produce the present fragmented and tense situation where anti-racist legislation exists side by side with persistent racial discrimination.

In this chapter I will be analysing racism from the 'two places' of the individual and the collective, and those of the psychological and the social. But in addition, I aim to stay conscious of the unconscious splitting that imposes a self and Other onto our experience and forces us into oppositional modes of thinking. In this case I will be using what Jung has to say about the function of opposites in the human psyche and the meaning of the incest symbol.

Racism: some definitions

Before I continue I need to clarify various points about my use of the word 'racism'. Firstly, I hold that 'race' itself is an empty category that cannot refer to any biological or genetic difference between peoples that is anything more than trivial. It is an often repeated point that there is far more individual difference within any delineated racial group than there are average differences between such groups.[4] Despite the superficiality of the visible differences between races in terms of skin colour and facial features, these take on huge importance as markers, and as the identifying characteristics (along with diet, dress and so on) that select a group out for discrimination and oppression. *It is the selection of a group for discrimination that constitutes racism*, not any inferiority constituted through appearance of difference the group may carry for the racist. The current wave of overt racism in the

United Kingdom is directed against immigrants from central Europe whose skin colour and clothing barely differs from those of the majority white population.

Secondly, this chapter is only concerned with the European people's (including those who now form the USA) political, economic and psychological development that has produced a particular type of racism in this epoch. I am sure that, elsewhere, other racisms always persist as they did at other times in the past, and these may be sensitive to other forms of analysis such as in *Purity and Danger*, for example, where Mary Douglas discusses group identity via dietary prohibitions.[5] Having said this, racism persisting in other parts of the world, apparently unconnected to the European experience, can often be found to have direct links back to colonial times. It may also be linked to the contemporary influence exerted through the World Bank and aid agencies. It was a well-known strategy of European colonisation to use existing divisions, discriminations and enmities in the indigenous populations to foster greater overall control despite a relatively minimal white presence. Franz Fanon analyses this as the 'racial distribution of guilt' which stems from the whites and moves between ethnic groups such as Jew-Arab, Asian-Negro, African-Caribbean.[6] In this view Fanon emphasises the hegemony of a world system dominated by white Europeans, even when the Europeans are no longer present in person. The distinction between racism in a universalistic and a non-universalistic epoch is commented on by Joel Kovel who notes that only in the former does the cruelty and domination between peoples penetrate into the 'essence of personhood' that we see in slavery and the Holocaust.[7]

Lastly, and central to my argument, I believe there is much more to racism in European culture than its gross expression in openly racist views and actions. *Racism is part of the sustained splitting of the human psyche that constitutes modernity and everyday life.* By participating in the culture we participate in racism despite our individual position. Evidence for this can be found in facts such as the continuing under-representation of non-white people in professional positions and as university students relative to the population; the over-representation of non-whites in lower paid and service jobs; and the over-representation of non-white males, as unemployed, in prison, excluded from school or diagnosed with serious mental illness. This distortion could not occur except through ideologies, resting on unconscious processes and conscious ideation, that mark non-whites as inferior and circumscribe their freedom to enter the dominant culture without its permission.

Psychoanalysis and racism

Earlier psychoanalytic attempts at an analysis of racism were characterised by a reductive approach that took little account of the social context or historical aspects of racism, as though it could be understood in intrapsychic or developmental terms alone.[8] In such studies, racism tended to be reduced to the projection and displacement of infantile hatred, hostility or disgust, with the focus restricted to the dynamics of the instincts and to dynamics within the family.

Franz Fanon, writing in the late 1960s, holds views that develop the psychoanalytic perspective more in the direction of this chapter. He criticizes Mannoni's[9] mistaken view that the responsibility for racism lies with 'racists'. Mannoni expresses it as: 'European civilization and its best representatives are not, for instance, responsible for colonial racism; that is the work of petty officials, small traders, and colonials who have toiled much without great success'.[10] By reducing the problem to one of individuals, Mannoni's view fails to grasp the bigger psychological and historical point of the linkage between racism and the psyche of modernity. In criticising this more or less reductive psychoanalytic position, Fanon refers to the collective unconscious as the location of contemporary, as well as ancient, collective contents such as 'the myth of the bad nigger'[11] previously mentioned, while also emphasising that 'there are inner relationships between consciousness and the social context'.[12]

The psychoanalytical point in this analysis is that racism is seen as a defence against an unbearable sense of alienation which has arisen as a condition of modern life. What is key about this account of racism is that the analysis has moved on from the personal experience (for example, in terms of family dynamics) towards an attempt to take into account the modern social context. As Stephen Frosh puts it, these views carry the notion that 'racism is a manifestation of flight from the experience of modernity'.[13]

I broadly agree with Fanon's views, but in writing from a Jungian perspective I find important differences. In psychoanalytic theorising, the dynamics of social collective behaviour tend to be explained in terms of the dynamics of the ego and id, on the one hand, and the dynamics within the nuclear family on the other. Psychoanalytic accounts of racism seem dominated by the presence of individual dynamics, which are then generalised to form the 'social' effect – or, in other words, collective dynamics are being treated as if they are reducible to the dynamics of individuals. I find this psychoanalytic approach demonstrated in the constant reference to 'racists' (especially in Frosh[14] and Rustin[15]), the actors in society who apparently carry the racism and cause it to be a troubling factor. What this perspective misses is the degree to which racism is not the 'passion' (to use Sartre's word) of certain individuals or groups, but is part of the ground of modernity. As individuals, 'racists' are more about the violence, aggression and hatred that is being expressed; they are using racism as a vehicle which provides a circumscribed, clearly defined 'Other', and a target for their animosity. My point is that a Freudian approach will always tend to refer to the individual in explaining the social form of human being because its tools of analysis are restricted to the dynamics of individuals. By contrast, a Jungian psychological approach has the conceptual advantage of recognising a collective unconscious within the individual psyche, and *this collective unconscious is reproduced by and also produces new instances of collective social phenomena*. The individual and the collective aspects of our human being are brought together in this model of our minds which provides a way of thinking about the dynamics between the individual and the collective, the psychological and the social, that is *already located in a dynamic interplay within each individual*. In addition, the concept of the collective unconscious directly addresses the reality of a political and cultural dynamic as a force in itself. Beyond the individual 'racists', racism itself is a ubiquitous collective force that is not only visible and obvious but is also *a hidden presence and an expression of the split psyche of modernity*.

The split between self and the (racial) other

But how does this split continue to reproduce over generations? And, historically, how does such a powerful structuring of our human being arise in the first place? To address the first question, it has struck me how young children up to about 6 practically never remark on the racial difference of other children, but at 9 can be as racist and biased as an adult. This suggests to me two things: firstly, that the developing infant only takes on as much 'otherness' as it can manage at a time. Indeed, research on neurological capacities early in life suggests that the brain paces its capacities for knowing the Other. Research shows that newborn babies are 'actively and effectively avoidant of experiences, and this is particularly noticeable in unfamiliar circumstances'.[16] Once established at the stage of 'object constancy', the infant's cognitive and emotional capacity for knowledge of otherness constructs a hierarchy of significant others with parents and family as the 'others' closest to self. It is not long before social and cultural influences impose a further hierarchy of otherness via ideology and learning.

It seems to me that when we make distinctions of otherness the *distance of Other from self* and the *distance between the others* will be conditioned by certain parameters. Firstly, the cognitive and emotional capacity to register the distinction. Secondly, the range of others available, and thirdly how they are valued or put in order of importance. This is where we have to shift into social theorising – the collective culture will set the priorities and range of its Other according to prevailing beliefs and values handed down at the family level and the wider level of education and media communications. Different contexts or questions will determine where is self or where is other. In this, the *need and desire* of the individual or the culture – which will vary in both cases and from time to time – becomes important. This is a central and complex factor, which this chapter as a whole is trying to address. To put it crudely for now, the creation of the Other followed by the consequences of *dealing with* the Other, the not-I, leads to discomfort and restlessness in human beings; it results in an energy that is always seeking resolution in action and rationality. It is the motor of our present consciousness and creates serious limitations on alternative developments.

The paradigm of self and Other is useful in considering how racism grew and now persists in modern times. My main point, which I pick up later when I return to theorising on opposites, is that the paradigm of self and Other replaces and attempts to compensate for a more fundamental dualism or split: that between the unconscious and the conscious mind. Considered historically, the last 500 years of European civilisation have seen a consolidation in the breakdown of dialogue between the conscious and the unconscious – frequently depicted as the gulf between 'man' and 'nature'. Early on, this psychological condition was enacted in the political world by elite classes wrenching instrumental power from the Church, and hence from God, and thereby legit-imising their new rationalism. Instead of man being the object of God, the material world could be created as the object of man – to achieve, in Schiller's phrase, the 'de-godding of nature'. Through this nature could 'be capable of human use and control according to human whim and desire, and Europeans, uniquely as far as we know, among all cultures could assume, in Descartes' words, that humans were the masters and possessors of nature'.[17]

This objectifying of the world in the service of instrumental rationality, this creation of the exploitable Other, provided the psychological basis for the expansion of Europeans and

Figure 7.1   1492: Conquest of Paradise (Due West-Legend-Cyrk/The Kobal
Collection)

what we now experience as modernity. It is easy to see how
the state of mind that viewed new lands purely in terms of
what wealth could be appropriated for use back in Europe,
would extend this attitude to the native populations encountered. In this way the European invader was able to view
fellow human beings as just more objects of nature ripe for
a justified exploitation. The binoculars of secular pragmatism
freed European adventurers of any moral constraint that
might have provided a human connection and thus interrupted their ruthless exploitation.

The Enlightenment shift from will of God to the will of
human reason justified the nation state and its newly
capitalised adventurers in the creation and exploitation of
an Other in the form of the populations and resources
of far-away lands. The chronicles of Christopher Columbus
reveal in expressive detail the psychological attitude of
one individual of the time, which tends to confirm the collective historical perspective. In writings dating from his
voyages between 1492 and 1502, Admiral Cristóbal Colón,

111

Christopher Columbus, reveals the ramshackle beginnings of such successful exploitation but also typifies the rapidly established racist attitudes that made it possible. When encountering the Taino people on his first landing in 1492, Columbus remarked on their simplicity and friendliness in terms that would later produce notions of the 'noble savage' in the European imagination. But he immediately presumed the Taino as inferior, 'not merely because [a sure enough sign] they were naked, but because [his society could have no surer measure] they seemed so technologically backward'. 'Very poor in everything', he wrote, 'they have no iron'.[18] Their pleasant, welcoming nature was also treated cynically with 'they ought to be good servants . . . I will carry six off at my departure',[19] and 'They are fit to be ordered about and made to work . . . no Christian need do a hand's turn of work in the Indies'.[20] In this way slavery was born, not intentionally though any rational plan, but as the accidental result of a tribute system so cruelly and ham-fistedly enforced that it rapidly disintegrated into full enslavement as the Spanish continued to pursue further gains requiring further control of the population.

Such ruthlessness led to the fleeing of natives as the colonies began to establish themselves under the Spanish. Natives only fled to live in the hills once the colonists had destroyed their villages and social cohesion. Despite the fact of the natives' long established social organisation their retreat to the 'wilds' enabled the formation and sanctioning of the negative European image of the native as 'savage beast'. The noble savage, on the other hand, was a Romantic characterisation of the native created as a positive opposite to the sophisticated European. The noble savage was fantasised as a human individual free of the need of interfering government because he was himself free of crime and greed and living in harmony. It is ironic that the noble savage should have 'provided the underlying characteristics of the free commonwealth',[21] a Utopian future for a degenerated Europe in the New (Other) World when such an image was always entwined with that of the savage beast. As Sale says, this latter view of the native took over, 'as soon as anything of real value was seen in the new lands that were inconveniently in the hands of the natives'[22] and especially after Cortes discovered gold in 1519.

Machiavelli, in 1513, through to Galileo in 1632 and Descartes in 1637 and 1641, produced, despite the tenuous grip of Rome, the intellectual and philosophical texts that foreshadowed modernity and began to formalise the necessary split between psyche and the material world. Intellectual expansion followed on from political expansion and economic success and eventually the eighteenth century saw a 'period of great and exaggerated admiration for the observation of matter and nature'.[23] Nature objectified as Other was established in the *Encyclopedia* (written between 1751 and 1764) which was designed to replace Thomas Aquinas' *Summa Theologica*, and extended European man's mapping of the world previously contoured by God and the Catholic Church.

In America, the Declaration of Independence, on 4 July 1776, was based on John Locke's 'social contract'. The thinking behind this, although inspired by the Utopian image of the noble savage, was purely for the bourgeoisie to refute the sovereign being able to put himself above the law. Despite stating that, 'all men are created equal and are endowed by their Creator with certain inalienable rights . . . life, liberty and the pursuit of happiness' the Declaration was far from a liberal distribution of power to the masses. The emphasis on bringing the sovereign within the fully secular realm of government is a continuation of the epoch's earlier steps in reducing the power of the Catholic Church. And the blatant hypocrisy of its wording in the context of colonial slavery and the genocide of Native Americans only underlines how simultaneous and integral to this development of 'civilisation' racism has been.

This is the historical and cultural trajectory of modernity, but what of its psychology? I now approach this via a consideration of Jung's theories of the shadow and the opposites.

The shadow

The last few pages have underlined the construction of self and Other where the Other is made inferior with a consequent superiority accruing to self. So much is evident in the case of racism. As Paul Gordon quotes, 'By attributing a population with certain characteristics in order to categorise and differentiate it as Other, those who do so establish criteria by which they themselves are represented . . .'.[24] In other words, the construction of the Other as inferior summarises the characteristics that the self does not want to have. At the level of individual psychology, this is how Jung defined the shadow: as 'the thing a person has no wish to be'[25] and, 'the less it is embodied in the individual's conscious life, the blacker and denser it is'.[26] As an archetype, the shadow's contents contain powerful affects which can be projected, and within his theory, 'Jung found a convincing explanation not only of personal antipathies but also the cruel prejudices and persecutions of our time'.[27]

Therefore, it has been all too easy to view racism as a mass projection by the dominant white culture onto the black population by which the whites have identified a group to carry their shadow. This level of explanation can be useful, especially in certain areas. I am thinking of the themes of materiality and sexuality where the shadow of capitalist acquisitiveness and greed gets projected as black criminality, and the shadow of instinctive sexuality gets projected onto the black male as 'rapist' and onto non-white women as exotically seductive.

However, I find this 'explanation' inadequate and reductive – leaving me with a sense of 'so what?' Presumably for psychotherapy, 'owning' or 'coming to terms with' shadow contents should remove or reduce the power of such projections. The snag is, to pursue the example I have chosen, that we are human beings in an epoch and a culture where material acquisitiveness and control of sexuality are not optional. They are facts of our social and psychological existence and so too are the projections that go with them. It is also no accident that there are groups available to receive such projections. *The history that makes one also made the other*.

The trouble with theorising about the shadow is that we get seduced by the ego-shadow *split*. Jung was aware of this when he emphasised: 'the essential thing is not the shadow but the body which casts it',[28] and also that: *'les extrèmes se touchent* . . . Our mistake lies in supposing that the radiant things are done away with by being explained from the shadow side'.[29] In other words, substance and shadow are two indivisible aspects of a single phenomenon. They coexist in such a way that, from the point of view of shadow theorising, the prospect for change looks pessimistic.

I need now to call back the paradigm of the self-Other split and hold it up, as it were, like a transparency through which to view shadow theorising and the theory of opposites. What is immediately noticeable as a difference between the shadow theory and opposites theory is that, in the former, the Other is necessarily rejected and negatively valued to preserve the superiority and 'rightness' of the self. But, as I pointed out in Chapter 2, in the theory of opposites the two sides are sustained in ambivalence, the tension of the contradiction is tolerated. When tolerance of this ambivalence breaks down a split occurs and I am maintaining that *shadow theorising only accounts for this moment, namely the splitting*. For a deeper explanation of self and Other, and racism, historically and psychologically, we need to pursue the theory of opposites.

The opposites and the `conjunctio`

In *The Political Psyche*, Andrew Samuels recommends a wariness of 'excessive dependence on complementarity, on the dogma of 'the opposites', on oppositional thinking, and, above all, on essentialism'.[30] He states:

It is not enough to simply accept or reject 'the opposites'. We have to try and make a psychological theory about them so as to explain their immense psychopolitical power. We have to try to explain how opposites such as

Jew/German, homosexual/heterosexual, black/white, female/male, thinking/feeling actually work on the cultural level. What kind of profound split in humanity and human ideation is being carried by these opposites? . . . If we make a psychological theory that explains some of these political issues, then we might be better placed to examine, and dispute, what is really meant by 'marginal'.[31]

Jung maintained 'the opposites are the ineradicable and indispensable preconditions of all psychic life'.[32] By definition, a theory of opposites refers to opposing, irreconcilable forces coexisting in the psyche or the Jungian self (that is, the whole conscious-unconscious mind). There is a sense here of an opposition similar to the 'self and Other' I have been referring to, but in this formulation it is located *within the self*. As I have said, the idea of the shadow is attractive to an analysis of racism because racism always involves defining the Other as inferior, and thus helps to achieve (affectually and politically) the unambivalent definition of a 'superior' self. But viewed from the perspective of a theory of opposites, it may be said that by splitting off parts of the self and projecting them onto a perceived Other, as happens in racism, what occurs is not so much a defining of self and Other, but *a denying of the self*. By which I mean a denial in the sense of the self's potential for fuller, deeper, psychological experience through *dialogue with itself*; this is epitomised by the dialogue, or intercourse, or *conjunctio* between the conscious mind and the unconscious. From the point of view of the self this intercourse is a meeting of *like with like*. Contradictorily, at the same time, to the ego-conscious mind it is a potentially threatening collision of opposites.

The incest symbol

I will now amplify these ideas by considering the relationship between the function of the incest symbol, the historical belief in cannibalism and the role of marginality in late modernity.

What links these is, of course, the theme of *like with like* and its opposite – the theme of the *like-unlike*, or *self-Other split*.

I chose the word 'dialogue' when referring to the relationship between the conscious mind and the unconscious. Jung uses the word 'union' as he points out how 'Incest symbolises union with one's own being, it means individuation or becoming a self . . . Incest is simply the union of like with like'.[33] Incest is, on one level, a concrete social form of sexual behaviour, which is disapproved, regarded as wrong and is subject to a universal taboo. However, on the non-concrete, symbolic level (such as we might find in dreams or mythology), incest offers a nurturing symbol of inner communication. Incest appears to qualify as a part of our human being that exists in two places – the 'external' social-cultural sphere and the 'internal' psychological sphere of our being. To explain this point of view, Jung cites Layard's anthropological work on tribal groups whose social practices result in the organisation of the group into two lineage halves. Then, by organising marriages between the cross-cousins of the two lineages (father's daughter of one lineage marrying father's brother's son of the other, for example) the benefits of both endogamy and exogamy are retained. Exogamy, or marrying 'outside the group' or 'with the unlike' benefits by reducing risks which may arise from inbreeding at the individual level, and by expanding the cooperative links in land and livestock ownership and use at the social level. Endogamy, quasi-incestuous marrying 'within the group' or 'like with like', benefits by keeping ownership and loyalties intact but can result in stagnation of the gene pool and land use which groups had noticed were ultimately destructive.

This tactic of small-scale human groups is cited as evidence of social organisation responding to the incest instinct. Not only does the social group achieve the closest marriage system short of incest itself (cousins are one step away from brothers and sisters), but Jung finds a psycho-spiritual significance in Layard's understanding of the cross-cousin marriage system. 'He [Layard] regards the endogamous [incest] tendency as a genuine instinct which if denied realization in the flesh, must realize itself in the spirit. Just as the exogamous order made culture possible in the first place, so also it contains a latent spiritual purpose.'[34]

As this system of human organisation evolves with the expansion of population, the exogamous 'marrying out' aspect of the system expands while the endogamous tendency is repressed. It is not possible for the concrete, lived social form (exogamous marriage) to exist without its hidden psychological counterbalance which now lives underground in the form of an unconscious mental process. Following this, 'The conscious personality with its one-track (exogamous) tendency comes up against an invisible (endogamous) opponent, and because this is unconscious it is felt to be a stranger and therefore manifests itself in a projected form'.[35] Historically, it makes its appearance first in human figures – political leaders, kings and queens who 'have the power to do what others may not do',[36] but also shifted to the sphere of the gods (as this was the source of kingly power): 'The endogamous tendency finds an outlet in the exalted sphere of the gods and in the higher world of the spirit' Jung writes.[37] In doing so he provides evidence for the way in which our human psyche has evolved from its beginnings in instinctive forces (sex and procreation) to produce a life of the spirit on the highest level and has done so by adopting practical strategies which are not individual or biological but *cultural forces enacted at the collective level of human society.*

But what about the cultural organisation of the Enlightenment and modernity? What happens in the historical case of cultural developments that, firstly, deny the link between rulers and the gods (in other words, deny the 'divine right of kings') and unlink human purpose and will from the 'will' of a creator God? This, of course, is exactly what occurred in the epoch under scrutiny. The Christian Church, corrupted by its own secular materiality and no longer a viable container for the spirit, could not continue, as it once had done, to supply a cultural form needed for the projection Jung describes. Earlier 'pagan' containers of the old religions, folk wisdom and magical belief had already come under attack by Christianity and, apart from in the margins, reached the point of extinction under Enlightenment rationality.

To summarise, modern discourse on racism focuses on the Other, but the apparent hatred and rejection of the Other can be viewed as a refusal or inability to proceed further in psychological growth – an opting for a restrictive 'cult of consciousness'. Ironically, the Other perceived in the racially differentiated can be viewed as an *alikeness* – a projected property of the self that when encountered under particular cultural and individual psychological conditions strikes chords of incestuous possibilities and a fear of the depth, danger and threat to the conscious self which personal spiritual advance could entail.

Incest and cannibalism

I have already mentioned the Jung-Layard theory of the incest instinct being projected as a prerogative of the gods. Alongside this, cannibalism has also been regarded as the gods' prerogative and is mentioned in Greek and other myths. Marina Warner maintains that 'incest figures as a form of metaphorical cannibalism: eating your own',[38] the link being, again, the union of like with like. Warner does not explore the psychological implications of this but her piece as a whole is very useful for the links I am making between racism, incest and modernity.

Cannibalism as an image can be viewed as part of the same problem that the incest symbol carries; at one level is the tension of the endogamy/exogamy position, and at a further level the tension of the opposites – specifically, the tension between conscious and unconscious processes in the self. At the same time, cannibalism as an image or as a human practice exists in the minds of humans as a material belief which is central to the racism of this epoch. Let me illustrate.

On his first sighting of the Indies on Columbus' second voyage, Coma, on board with Columbus writes, 'These islands are inhabited by *Canabilli*, a wild unconquered race which feeds on human flesh. I would be right to call them *anthropophagi*'.[39] For centuries Europe had heard about strange tribes of maneaters. Seen as violaters of the Lord's natural law by which 'higher' orders were expected to eat only 'lower' ones, the anthropophagi were in the forefont of a pantheon of monsters. So when Columbus understood from his friendly Taino Indians that there was a fierce tribe of *Caribas* (the name from which Europeans got *Canibas*, then cannibal) in other islands, he encouraged the myth of the cannibal. As Sale says, 'Whenever the people of an island were . . . non-hostile, the Spanish declared that they were the Tainos . . . and whenever they were deemed to be hostile, or at least defensive, they were said to be the warlike Carib, the bad Indians'.[40] Originally imposed by the Europeans, the myth then becomes embedded in subsequent European chronicles and history as 'fact'. This is in spite of that fact that there is no anthropological evidence or adequate documentation of cannibalism as a custom in any society, including that of 'the very aborigines who name now means maneaters'.[41] The clue to the meaning of the belief in cannibals lies in the discourse of the Other, in this case the savage beast. 'Reports of cannibalism provided the means of justifying the enslavement and deportation of these creatures so clearly beyond the pale of God's favour that they could rightly be regarded as beasts . . . the myth . . . permitted the denigration, and thus the conquest and exploitation, of peoples whose lands were seen as increasingly desirable in European eyes.'[42]

This is surely no shadow projection, but points to a more fundamental split in the psyche where, having begun to loosen ties to God and Church, the European psyche can itself behave like God in *re-creating man*. Human rational thought, not the Word of God as delivered by Bible and Church, asserted a right to define what was human and what was the non-human, bestial Other. Conscious rationality thereby defined its own world order and established the psychological conditions for European expansion and conquest.

Marina Warner points out how the cannibal myth is often reinforced with 'they eat their own children', which super-imposes incest and cannibalism and underlines a connection both psychological and cultural. All of this supports the idea of a split in psyche arising from the loss of true religious forms with the result that symbols plummet from the gods down into a debased worldly form. Moreover, the secularisation of the symbol does not follow on as just one effect of a debased culture, it is more important than that. The loss of the symbolic is *the psychological force* that energises the social collective and allows a particular form of rela-tionship with, and belief about, 'the world' to progress. It is characterised by detachment, utilitarianism and exploitation. The linkage between the incest symbol and the cannibal myth brings home the linkage between racism and our psycho-logical failure in this epoch: the failure to sustain a dialogue between the conscious and unconscious mind.

The margin

We need to find a position 'outside' the oppositional views, a position from which these very views can be addressed. We can designate this as the margin, the space off the page where critical notes and directions can be inscribed in preparation for the redrafting. As bell hooks writes, with direct reference to consciousness of racism, the margin is a site we should stay in to discover 'the possibility of radical perspective from which to see and create, to imagine alter-natives, new worlds'.[43] I agree with hooks when she notes how postmodern culture is particular for its ruptures and fragmentation which provide space for radical thinking, which can result in new and varied forms of bonding across groups and disciplines that have never previously been in dialogue: 'The overall impact of postmodernism is that many other groups now share with black folks a sense of deep alienation, despair, uncertainty, loss of sense of grounding even if it is not informed by shared circumstance. Radical postmodernism calls attention to those shared sensibilities.'[44]

121

This is exactly what Samuels is referring to when he urges us to 'take our sense of fragmentation, fracture and complexity as *healing* as well as wounding to a sense of political and social empowerment'.[45] On the same page he refers to depth psychology as the precursor of late twentieth-century resacralisation,[46] thus indicating its potential to subvert the dominant elements in the individual and the collective culture, by being able to address what is most fundamental in the psyche of modernity. Racism especially can benefit from an analysis that employs the healing potential of fragmentation and complexity by finding a site of expression in the margin, between the fragments. The aim is not to achieve a spurious (and false) wholeness, however, but to gain insight through seeing what can be found in the fragments as they are reflected in each other.

But within texts on race and cultural politics, the margin can be used as a site to keep the racially Other situated where their voice is silenced by the centre or dominant culture which says: 'No need to hear your voice. Only tell me about your pain. I want to know your story. And then I will tell it back to you in a new way'.[47] But hooks goes on to emphasise that marginality is more than a site of deprivation, 'it is a site of radical possibility, a space of resistance . . . a central location for the production of counter-hegemonic discourse that is not just found in words but in habits and the way one lives'.[48] This then, for all its romantic idealism, is the importance of the margins – those places in society where the non-conformist, the critical, the excluded and the non-qualifying subsist, often in deprivation but with a particular advantage. It is in this site of marginality, the tectonic pressures that sustain a split psyche, keeping the unconscious from dialogue with consciousness and maintaining dualistic paradigms and divisive ideation are at their weakest.

Modernity: the conclusion?

The span of modernity over the last 500 years is coterminous with the disintegrating of psyche, beginning with the material-spiritual splits in culture and politics, and then within the economics, philosophy and science of these centuries. This has been developed and reproduced through succeeding forms: mechanisation and the advance of industrialisation, and later the globe-shrinking power of air and space travel and the revolution in communications that information technology has produced.

For Jung, these conditions of modernity, 'increasing internationalism and the weakening of religion',[49] have resulted in the modern phenomenon of the mass-man for which there is 'but one remedy: the inner consolidation of the individual who is otherwise threatened with inevitable stultification and dissolution in the mass psyche'.[50] Marshall Berman's description of modernity from the sociological point of view would ring true at every stage of the epoch: 'To be modern is to find ourselves in an environment that promises us adventure, power, joy, growth, transformation of ourselves and the world and, at the same time, that threatens to destroy everything we have, everything we know, everything we are'.[51]

The British psychologist Stephen Frosh holds the view that within the racist psyche is a 'repudiation of modernity, of multiplicity and heterogeneity. Racist ideology is the building of a fort . . . to defend . . . the integrity of the disintegrated self'.[52] What is of note in this point of view is the emphasis on racism as a 'fort' – that is, a defence. I am in disagreement with this in that my own emphasis is on racism as an *attack*. It is defensive against fragmentation, for sure, but it is not a passive retreat behind the walls of a fortified defence. It is an active, destructive attack on the *conjunctio*, an attack on the potentially healing dialogue within the psyche. Frosh's image of the racist's fort stems from imagining the racist's image of an all-white 'golden age' that racism is defending itself against and trying to preserve, or rather, *restore*. There has never been such an age of homogeneity and wholeness. *Modernity, as a psychological mode, has always required a split psyche*, an Other to be the object of its instrumentality. This is why racism forms an integral element in the split-sustaining process that is modernity. By becoming conscious of this aspect of its function we may be able to address it, but only side by side with addressing similar functions – involving discriminations on the basis of gender, physical ability, sexual orientation and so on – that sustain our condition.

Peter Homan's analysis of Jung's psychology in the context of modernity reminds us how, due to Jung's personal experiences and his sensitivity to the times he lived through, 'Jung rendered normative a lack of meaning in the social sphere'[53] and, 'In the world of Jung's thought, the mind became society and church – a world within a world'.[54] This warns us that psychological and psychoanalytic views run the risk of collapsing the two places of the social and the psychological into one mental space. However, it also demonstrates the point that modernity, with its inadequate symbolic and spiritual forms and its emphasis on materiality and instrumental rationality, is going to lead to such a collapse into the psychological as we try and find our way out of what we have created. Jung's emphasis on symbolic forms, like incest, contribute to 'demodernisation' as Homans understands it,[55] by which he means a challenge to modernity and a resistance from the margin. This reminds us that, despite a degree of legitimisation achieved through alliances with medicine and other establishment disciplines, depth psychology, because of its attention to *unconscious processes, will always speak from the margin*. Possession of such a voice from the margin enables the critique of modernity that depth psychology can, and should, offer in the service of healing.

But I do not pretend to offer any prescription for undoing racism. On the contrary, I have pointed out, rather pessimistically perhaps, how racism is embedded in the psyche and culture, maintaining material aspects of our lives and rationalising, based on unconscious splits in the psyche and the failure of a dialogue between the conscious and unconscious mind. This chapter, like others in this book, offers a global overview of a state of mind and culture that produces such splits and sustains a particular phase of our human being human. The unsatisfactoriness of our modern, mass lives and the reactive trend towards the narcissism it produces[56] provide a context for the popularity of ideas of turning inward for healing and individuation that are associated with Jungian and other psychologies and therapies. But we cannot eschew the social order for too long. Individuation cannot proceed without a relationship to the collective. To achieve a healing of split worlds and the dissolving of modernity's worst effects such as racism, our psychological attitude needs to find its place in the social and political order. Such a reconstruction will not be easy; there will be much resistance. Karl Marx once said of modern times, 'All that is solid melts into air, all that is holy is profaned, and men at last are forced to face . . . the real conditions of their lives and their relations with their fellow men'.[57] What he failed to add was that the most insidious elements have the highest melting point.

Notes

1 Cleaver, E. (1968) *Soul On Ice*. New York: Dell Distributing, p. 29.
2 Fanon, F. (1967) *Black Skin, White Masks*. New York: Grove Press, quoted in Brown, P. (1973) *Radical Psychology*. London: Tavistock, pp. 267–8.
3 Gordon, P. (1993) 'Souls in armour: thoughts on psychoanalysis and racism', *British Journal of Psychotherapy*, 10(1), p. 73.
4 For example, Plomin, P. (1994) 'Gene rebels with a cause', the *Independent*, 20 October.
5 Douglas, M. (1966) *Purity and Danger*. Harmondsworth: Penguin.
6 Fanon, op. cit.
7 Kovel, J. (1988) *The Radical Spirit*. London: Free Association Books.
8 For example, Sterba, R. (1947) 'Some psychological factors in negro race hatred'; Dollard, J. (1937) 'Caste and class in a southern town' and (1938) 'Hostility and fear in social life'; Orr (1946) 'Anti-semitism and the psychopathology of everyday life'; Hamilton (1966) 'Some dynamics of anti-negro prejudice', all described fully in Gordon, P. (1993) 'Souls in armour: thoughts on psychoanalysis and racism', *British Journal of Psychotherapy*, 10(1), pp. 62–76.
9 Mannoni, O. (1964) *Prospero and Caliban: Psychology of Colonisation*. New York: Praeger.
10 Ibid., p. 24.

11 Fanon, op. cit.

12 Ibid., p. 273.

13 Frosh, S. (1989) 'Psychoanalysis and racism', in Richards, B. (ed.) *Crises of the Self: Further Essays on Psychoanalysis and Politics*. London: Free Association Books, p. 235.

14 Ibid.

15 Rustin, M. (1991) *The Good Society and the Inner World*. London: Routledge.

16 Trevarthan, C. (1987) in R.L. Gregory (ed.) *The Oxford Companion to the Mind*. Oxford: Oxford University Press, p. 364.

17 Sale, K. (1992) *The Conquest of Paradise. Christopher Columbus and the Columbian Legacy*. London: Pan-Macmillan, p. 40.

18 Ibid., p. 96.

19 Ibid., p. 97.

20 Ibid., p. 112.

21 Ibid., p.200.

22 Ibid., p. 201.

23 Ibid., p. 50.

24 Miles, R. (1989) *Racism*, quoted in Gordon, op. cit., p. 39.

25 Jung, C.G. (1966) *The Collected Works*, Vol.16. London: Routledge & Kegan Paul, para. 470.

26 Jung, C.G. (1969) *The Collected Works*, Vol. 11. London: Routledge & Kegan Paul, para. 131.

27 Samuels, A. *et al.* (1986) *A Critical Dictionary of Jungian Analysis*. London: Routledge & Kegan Paul, p. 139.

28 Jung, C.G. (1966) *The Collected Works*, Vol. 16, London: Routledge & Kegan Paul, para.145.

29 Ibid., para.146.

30 Samuels, A. (1993) *The Political Psyche*. London: Routledge, p. 329.

31 Ibid., pp. 329–30.

32 Jung, C.G. (1970) *The Collected Works*, Vol. 14. London: Routledge & Kegan Paul, para. 206.

33 Jung, C.G. (1966) *The Collected Works*, Vol. 16. London: Routledge & Kegan Paul, para. 419.

34 Ibid., para. 458.

35 Ibid., para. 438. In reference to what has been said about the *shadow* earlier, please note that this statement confirms how the shadow is not the only way of understanding what gets 'projected' as the 'stranger'.

36 Ibid., para. 438.

37 Ibid., para. 439.

38 Warner, M. (1994) 'Beautiful beasts', the *Independent*, 17 February.

39 Sale, op. cit., p. 129.

40 Ibid., p. 131.

41 Ibid., p. 133.

42 Ibid., pp. 134–5.
43 hooks, b. (1991) *Yearning: Race, Gender and Cultural Politics*. London: Turnaround, p.150. bell hooks always spells her name using lower case, presumably as a way of signifying and reminding us of the margin from where she speaks.
44 Ibid., p. 27.
45 Samuels (1993), op. cit., p. 11.
46 Ibid.
47 hooks, op. cit., p. 152.
48 Ibid., p. 149.
49 Jung, C.G. (1966) *The Collected Works*, Vol. 16. London: Routledge & Kegan Paul, para. 443.
50 Ibid.
51 Berman, M. (1982) *All That is Solid Melts into Air: The Experience of Modernity*. New York: Simon & Schuster, p. 15.
52 Frosh, op. cit., p. 233.
53 Homans, P. (1979) *Jung in Context; Modernity and the Making of a Psychology*. Chicago: University of Chicago Press, p. 200.
54 Ibid., p. 201.
55 Ibid., p. 204.
56 See Lasch, C. (1979) *The Culture of Narcissism*. London: Abacus.
57 Marx, K. (1888) 'Speech at the anniversary of the *People's Paper*', in Tucker, R.C. (ed.) (1978) *The Marx-Engels Reader*, 2nd edn. New York: Norton, pp. 475–6.

What is the double when the original is gone?[1]

Set in ancient Japan, Kurosawa's film *Kagemusha* is the story of a criminal who bears a striking resemblance to a prominent warlord, Shingen. He is saved from punishment because he agrees to impersonate the warlord so as to confound the enemy and hide the fact that Shingen is dangerously wounded. The impersonation goes well while the lord is living, until we watch a desolate scene with a dilapidated hut on the shore of a lake from which hidden viewpoint the double witnesses the clandestine, water burial of the lord. He now realises he has to keep this knowledge secret even from the generals who employ him as no one is to know the lord is dead. The double realises that he is no longer a 'double' because the original is dead. He has no choice. He either 'is' the lord from now on, or he returns to his previous state as a condemned criminal.

Jonathan Glazer's film *Birth* is the story of Anna (played by Nicole Kidman), a thirty-something Upper East Side New Yorker whose husband Sean died ten years before. She is about to get remarried when a 10-year-old boy turns up on her doorstep and says, 'I am Sean. Do not marry that man.' What is she to think? Why is the child trying to claim he 'is' her dead husband? Just when she has recovered from the loss of the original Sean to get remarried, along comes a 'double' to remind her of her loss once again. While those around her dismiss the boy – who is also called Sean – Anna comes to believe that her dead husband has been reincarnated in this boy. For some time, Anna believes in the 'double' called Sean although the original Sean is gone.

Eventually, Anna does marry her new husband and the final scenes of the film show her being photographed. The wedding has taken place in an old mansion by the sea on the East Coast above Manhattan.[2] In itself we are reminded of Gatsby and his loss and regret. But in one shot we see Anna being photographed against a dilapidated hut away from the other guests.[3] The contrast between her beauty, her cream dress and the collapsed wooden building is moving and is reminiscent of the scene in *Kagemusha*. These last scenes show how Anna has not come to terms with the death of her husband Sean and the extent of her wish to believe in the 'double'. She has to grieve all over again or, rather, she has to complete a mourning she thought had ended. And what becomes of the double now the original has gone? We see the boy Sean being photographed too. He is merely one of many children being photographed in school for the school photo. The vast otherness of death and loss of the 'original' suggested by the burial in the water in *Kagemusha* gets echoed in the last scenes of *Birth*. Anna in her wedding dress rushes into the sea but she is held back by her new husband who has found her. The scene is bleak and heart-churning. The loss cannot be reversed. There is no double. The original has gone.

Notes

1 Where I have been struck by a recurring motif in two movies otherwise miles apart – *Kagemusha, The Shadow Warrior* (Kurosawa, 1980) and *Birth* (Jonathan Glazer, 2004).
2 The setting has echoes for me of Gatsby's mansion with its own associations of loss. The book, *The Great Gatsby* ends with lines I have always remembered, 'We beat on, boats against the current, being borne ceaselessly back into the past' (F. Scott Fitzgerald, 1925, *The Great Gatsby*. London: Penguin).
3 This scene was cut from the final print of *Birth* shown in the cinema. I was invited to view and comment on several earlier assemblies as the film was being edited and the scene was still included up to the very end. By the time you read this the DVD will be available and it may be included in the out-takes. Otherwise you will just have to take my word!

8

Trauma, memory and human being

The last chapters have been considering our human being from a broad perspective of collective culture and the span of history. I now wish to tighten the focus back onto the individual and a special aspect of our human being: our memory. In doing so I will be talking in a general sense about how we sustain our sense of identity through memory and how psychotherapy in particular pays attention to this function.

There are several aspects of memory and psychotherapy I will scan in this chapter. For a start, what are psychotherapists meant to do with memory in practice? Are they meant to dive in and revive lost parts of the self – sometimes referred to as repressed memories – assuming, like Freud originally did, that their restoration to consciousness will be healing? Freud's initial ideas maintained that conscious memory is affected by traumatic experience. Psychotherapies based on these ideas then make assumptions about memory and what psychotherapy needs to do to heal the mind and its symptoms such as dysfunction in relationships, fears and depression. One assumption is that the symptoms may have arisen because the mind has been damaged by traumatic experiences.

Psychotherapists allow themselves this assumption even if the individual has no memory of such trauma. Although it sounds irrational, it is theoretically possible for psychotherapy to claim that *because* a memory is absent, this is 'evidence' for a trauma that was severe enough for the mechanism of repression to banish it from conscious awareness. I will be picking up on the implications of this shortly.

Another question we need to ask is, what is the function of memory in consciousness? Is it a store – a warehouse – of everything we have learnt and experienced from the moment there were enough cells to form the self or soul we call 'me'? If so, then our sense of self will depend very much on the memories we retain – or, rather, what we manage to *select* and retain because we surely do not remember everything. Many studies have shown that memory cannot be a store like a filing cabinet ready to be opened and selected from. The psychologist Elizabeth Loftus describes memory as more like a bowl of clear water that gradually has drops of milk added until it forms a swirling opaqueness in which it is impossible to locate where each drop of milky memory has come from or is located.[1] It is also clear that recalled memories are reconstructions – not filing cabinet withdrawals – and, moreover, reconstructions that alter according to the circumstances and conditions at the time of recall. This makes us wonder where all the drops of memory have gone to. The warehouse idea likes to locate them in the wet stuff of the brain matter in our skulls, but other studies I will mention clearly show that the whole body of a person is vitally important to the conception of memory, where and what it is, how and why we recall, and the part it plays in making me 'me'.

This brings us to a third question: the issue of self-identity. If all goes well, our sense of ourselves remains fairly constant, even though we might occasionally say 'I forgot myself' when we find ourselves doing something regarded as 'out of character'. But for a person in a psychiatrically diagnosed state of fugue, forgetting oneself is a far more profound experience which can impact on the lives of those around. Some time before I had even considered training in psychotherapy, a friend of mine suffered the shock of discovering her husband had run off with another woman. My friend was only recently married and they had been planning to buy a house in a pretty town outside the city. She reacted to the news of his unfaithfulness by getting herself a train ticket one morning and travelling to the town where she booked herself into a hotel. She had little awareness of what she was doing until, late in the afternoon, she found herself staring into the hotel room mirror and realised she did not know who she was. She was naturally panicked and contacted the manager who called the police. Somehow she had rid herself of all her identifying documents and she had lost her memory of her real identity. This was before the time when credit cards were mandatory for booking into a hotel and she had booked herself in under the name of her husband's lover. Over several hours, talking with a helpful police detective helped my friend restore her memory of who she was and she returned home to be cared for by her parents. *Fugue* means 'flight'. She had fled from herself because that identity was linked to the overwhelming pain of being rejected by her husband. To cut herself off from the emotional pain, she had to cut herself off from all memory of the person who had experienced the pain.

My friend was able to return quite quickly to a sense of herself and begin to heal the damage. However, dissociated fracturing of the personality found in those suffering dissociative identity disorder proves far more difficult to treat and heal. Rather than the single soul or person we all assume ourselves to be, such people suffer from becoming someone else in a strangely complete way. For extended periods of time, little or none of the initial, familiar personality, identity or 'self' is present or remembered at all. The condition has been brought to public attention by many movies which depict dissociation in a very lop-sided fashion. Bates (played by Anthony Perkins), the murderer in Alfred Hitchcock's *Psycho* is depicted as a regular guy, if a little creepy, who, unaware of his condition, turns into a murderous monster when he assumes the female personality of his own (actually dead) mother.

Another movie character called Marnie in Hitchcock's film of the same name seems to be fully aware of herself when she is shown to be a compulsive thief who consciously disguises herself in each of her employments. However, when she will not have sex with her newly-wed husband (played by Sean Connery), he decides to find out why this is and what is troubling her. This leads to scenes where Marnie appears to lose her adult self and 'regress' into the personality of a small girl. All is revealed in classic Freudian fashion when it turns out she suffered a huge trauma at that age. Recall of the events helps her to heal her disturbed personality.

A recent movie by the Farelly brothers is even more misleading in its depiction of dissociation. In *Me, Myself and Irene*, Jim Carrey plays a character who is mild-mannered one minute but switches to a mean, aggressive and depraved character the next. The script is further misleading in its mis-use of the term 'schizophrenic' for his condition. Although this psychiatric term derives from two words that mean 'split mind', it has nothing to do with dissociation of the mind in the strict sense. Schizophrenic illness is one in which the person suffers from psychotic delusions of reality. These may take the form of hallucinations which are sometimes visual but more often heard as voices, and delusional fears of persecution such as being watched by the CIA or the television. Although some sufferers may experience delusions of omnipotence that they are St Joan, Jesus or Napoleon, this is more an expression of their illusory sense of power and importance rather than any loss of their personal identity. Carrey's character is not schizophrenic but he is 'split' between being a very *good guy* and a very *bad guy* in a cartoon-like way. To some extent he fits the picture of dissociated personality disorder better.

However, the movie needs to exaggerate the contrast between his two 'personalities' to achieve its dramatic, comic effect. This is enhanced by the way in which the 'good' personality has no recollection of the behaviour the 'bad' one gets up to. Actual cases in the psychiatric literature are not so clear cut but still show dramatic evidence for the power of the mind to forget and thus lose one personal identity and switch to another without the individual's knowledge.

133

I expect it is no coincidence that the Farrelly brothers set their film in Rhode Island, where they come from, and that they must have heard the famous case from the 1880s of Ansel Bourne[2] who one day, aged about 59, disappeared from his home in Coventry, Rhode Island. He had lost his first wife and was unhappily married to a second. He was last seen by a nephew he visited, had taken $551 out of the bank in Providence and then vanished. According to William James, who hypnotised Bourne in 1890, and pieced together the story:

> Two weeks later, a certain Albert Brown arrived at Norristown, Pennsylvania; he rented a little store, bought some merchandise and started a small business of stationery, confection, and small articles. [Two months later] On March 14th he woke up early in the morning and was completely disoriented. He had come back to his former personality of Ansel Bourne and was at a loss to understand what he was doing in this strange place. He called his neighbours, who thought he had become mentally deranged. Finally his nephew arrived . . . and took his uncle back to Coventry. Ansel Bourne had no recollection whatever of what he had done during the two months he had spent living under the name of Albert Brown.[3]

The secondary personality of Albert Brown was brought back under hypnotism. Brown knew nothing of Bourne, but gave a coherent account of what he had done during the two months of his existence, which, when checked, was found to be true. Why Brown did not notice the name of Ansel Bourne on his papers and chequebooks, and what preceded the return to his former personality is not recorded.

Since the nineteenth century, the psychiatric literature has been full of such cases. One of the most influential reports was published by Dr Morton Prince in 1900 and dealt with a case of more than two personalities in the one person – a so-called 'multiple personality'.[4] The woman, known by the pseudonym Christine Beauchamp, developed four distinct personalities as a result of a series of traumatic shocks. As personality B1 she was 23 years old and a student at a ladies college in New England. She had symptoms of hysterical origin such as headaches, insomnia and bodily aches and pains and felt a 'physical wreck'. In this personality she was very reserved and showed an exaggerated concern about the effects of her actions resulting in great inhibition. The second personality emerged when she was hypnotised by the doctor. He called the hypnotised Christine (known as B1) B2. B1 personality had no knowledge of B2 and what that person-ality said or felt but B2 knew all about B1. Then, under hypnosis again, B2 denied all knowledge of what she had said on a previous occasion, but when woken and re-hypnotised she apparently 'remembered' these statements. From this Prince discovered there was a further personality which came out under hypnosis which he called B3 and who called herself Sally. Sally was a complete contrast to the neurotic Christine B1 who:

> is a very serious-minded person, fond of books and study, of a religious turn of mind, and possesses a very morbid conscientiousness. She has a great sense of responsibility in life . . . is rather sad and depressed . . . the result of the general troubles and trials of her life. Sally on the other hand is full of fun, does not worry about anything; all life is one great joke to her; she hates books . . . does not like serious things, hates church – in fact is thoroughly childlike in every way.[5]

Sally (B3) knew all of Christine's thoughts while Christine (B1) knew nothing of Sally at all. When B1 became upset or exhausted Sally would emerge and might stay in existence a few minutes or a few hours. Sally hated Christine and although she would not wish to make anyone else unhappy she tormented Christine cruelly. For instance, knowing Christine was scared of snakes and spiders, Sally one day went to the countryside and collected some snakes and spiders, put them in a box addressed to Christine. When Christine (B1) 'opened the package they ran out and about the room and nearly sent her into fits'. Sally would also take a trip into the country a few miles by transport, shed her money and then 'wake up Miss Beauchamp who would find herself far out in the country with no means of getting home, no money and nothing for it but to walk. She had to beg rides when she could from passing wagons, and come back tired, worn out, used up for a week'. Sally's thoughts and memories were continuous with no gaps. Sally remembered things from the past that B1 knew nothing of at all and she wrote her own autobiography starting with her memories of being an infant in the cradle. As a small child she described liking the things that B1 did not like and vice versa.

However, Prince discovered that the B1 personality was not the original Christine Beauchamp, but one that had emerged just six years before as the result of a traumatic shock when a male friend turned up in the nurses' home where Christine had been training in Providence and who had frightened her by climbing a ladder and dramatically peering in through her window on a stormy night. B4 emerged when, six years later, during treatment of B1 with Dr Prince, Christine received a letter from this man and this threw her into shock again resulting in a further personality. This new personality had no knowledge of the time between seeing the man's face at the window and the present. She had no knowledge of who Dr Prince was or any familiarity with his consulting room, which she had been coming to for two years. She knew nothing of Christine's (B1) college or her new friends, and was like Rip Van Winkle who had no knowledge the world had moved on. Sally (B3) was an invaluable informant about the state of mind that B4 experienced. Dr Prince notes how the personality characteristics of B4 were very different from those of B1 or B3: 'she is irritable and quick-tempered, and resented as an impertinence – especially as she regarded most of us as strangers – any inquiry into her private thoughts and affairs'. However, although Sally had a mental life continuous with B4 (as she had with B1,

Christine), unlike with B1, Sally *did not know B4's thoughts*. Sally watched and observed B4 and concluded that the B4 personality knew nothing of the past six years: 'Why, she doesn't know anything, she is always fishing and guessing', she said and dubbed her 'The Idiot' – transferring her previous hatred for B1 onto B4 from this time.

Morton Prince concluded that neither B1 nor B4 were quite 'normal' and they both missed some of the attributes belonging to the original (pre-1893 and the traumatic event six years earlier) Christine Beauchamp. B1 seemed to be the result of a certain disintegration whereby the original personality became fractured and modified. But B1 was closer to the pre-traumatised Christine than B4. B4 had none of the taste for music, literature and religion and no 'emotionability' except for her bad temper.

But do you remember there was a B2 mentioned earlier in this narrative? What of her? Well, it turns out that B2 (the personality that emerged from Christine B1 when she was first hypnotised) was a combination of B1 and B4. B2 knew the thoughts of both B1 and B4 and said she was one, then the other, and then agreed she was both of them. Prince concluded that the 'real' Miss Beauchamp was a combination of B1 and B4 (sadly, the least happy and most inhibited characters) and Sally, B3, had little place in this composite. When the new combination of B1 and B4 gained strength, through Dr Prince's treatment, Sally tended to sink back out of sight to, as she put it, 'where I came from'. Dr Prince states, in the mechanistic language of the time, 'it must be that there exists normally some kind of physiological mechanism which allows disintegration to occur, and that normally, *within certain limits*, such disintegration is constantly occurring as a part of the mechanism of normal cerebration. In hysteria this physiological mechanism is carried to an extreme and pathological degree.' Morton Prince anticipates what has since become a contemporary view of human personality as consisting of several aspects of 'self'.

Although the experience of having contrasting and competing personalities in the one physical body must be disturbing, it is just as disturbing how these aspects of being a person are evaluated and treated. From the Morton Prince case, it can be seen that some of the personality traits were more approved of than others. Such an evaluation clearly depended on the beliefs and values of the time and place where Prince and Christine Beauchamp were living. This was the North Eastern United States at the end of the Victorian era where women's behaviour and freedom were circumscribed and limited far more than they are today. What we notice about the contrasting attributes of B1 and Sally (B3) can be found in many other reports of dissociated personality in women in this era. Quiet, compliant, domestically-based tastes and activities are approved of, while extroverted, adventurous, light-hearted and challenging traits are disapproved of. These are regarded as not appropriate to young women but acceptable in a young man. Yet the women concerned had, like their modern counterparts, the same potential for a far wider range of living and acting in life had they been allowed the chance. Only over subsequent years, as the result of economic and political change and protest, have women in general expressed themselves in a wider variety of ways of thought and action. It is no surprise that hysterical symptoms and cases of multiple personality in women have diminished in our time. While women are still somewhat restricted and not treated with full equality in modern industrial societies, the culture now allows a far greater range of personal attributes and activities compared to the Victorian era. These days, the psychological self-protection of the personality by dissociation no longer arises except in extreme cases of traumatic abuse.

Any human being's ability to live out their life in the fullest expression of their human potential depends not only on their inherent personal characteristics and local opportunities: it also depends on the cultural environment supporting and not denying such an expression of their humanity. It strikes me that the phenomena of dissociating and forgetting parts of the personality that we see in such cases as Christine Beauchamp arise as a result of the cultural conditions as much as anything to do with the individual person concerned. Different eras give rise to different opportunities to express one's humanity – just as they give rise to different pathologies, which are the result of not being allowed to 'be oneself'. As is often the case, psychopathologies allow us to reconsider and appreciate 'normal' psychological states, which, thankfully, most of us enjoy for most of the time.

There is a child's definition of memory that goes, 'My memory is the thing I forget with'.[6] As we will see, this childlike statement is deeper than we might first imagine. Due to the prevailing image of psychotherapy which stems from Freud's original methods, folk often come into psychotherapy with a powerful expectation that they are there to remember their historical past as far as they can recall it – or reconstruct it if they can't. Although current daily relationships are brought up for discussion, many clients and their therapists themselves expect to be paying special attention to the emotional tone of the events and relationships of their childhood. The here and now relationship with the therapist is also shown to be a source of insight and of healing but often only inasmuch as it reflects important aspects of early relationships which are being replayed in the so-called 'transference' to the psychotherapist. The psychodynamics of the client's present-day relationships tend to get reduced to this emphasis on early life. The bias towards childhood and early memories arises from a particular aspect of psychotherapy, which has been promoted in the general culture as it lay at the heart of Freud's first psychoanalytic formulations. As the depth psychology of the unconscious developed throughout the twentieth century, therapists such as Melanie Klein and Donald Winnicott took their interest in the development of children's psychology, applied it to adults and thus compounded the past-and-childhood way of understanding our normal and abnormal psychology.

But, if we look at the actual roots of this approach in Freud's cases, the recalled memories his patients reported and free-associated did not necessarily stem from the patient's childhood but were often derived from closer in time to the clinical present. In one case, the patient recalled how her father's friend had attempted to kiss her, and in another case, a young woman revealed the fear and anxiety which had arisen from tending to her dying father. While they were not recalled from childhood, these were always memories of a highly emotional nature and tended to reveal material in conflict with how the patient preferred to see herself.

Of course, Freud originally formulated his theory and technique by claiming that hysterical symptoms in his patients had their causes in early childhood trauma, usually involving the sexual abuse of the child by a male family member. Although we now know that childhood sexual abuse is far from uncommon and often connected with mental health difficulties in life, the idea was very unpopular with the psychiatric establishment of Freud's day and he swiftly abandoned what has become known as his 'seduction theory' of hysteria. Instead, he hypothesised that his patients' recall and reconstructions of memories were in fact fantasies in the patient's mind and universal to our psychology. Despite this, the role of memory and its restoration to consciousness persisted in lying at the heart of psychoanalytic treatment and still influences to a greater and lesser extent all the psychotherapy that is practised today.

But, by way of contrast, what was the psychiatric emphasis on memory just before Freud? While Freud abandoned hypnosis and recommended a free association of ideas through the 'talking cure' to achieve the restoration of lost memories, at the famous Salpetriere Hospital in Paris in the 1890s, Pierre Janet healed patients' symptoms in a fashion that was the complete reverse: he hypnotised them into believing the events that had precipitated the symptoms had never occurred. He deliberately cultivated deceptive memory. One poor woman, Marie, had been traumatised by her terror of her first menstrual period and standing in a barrel of freezing water in order to stop it. Her periods did cease for a while, but later she suffered from a 'hysterical hypothermia, terrible fits of freezing cold every month'[7] and other hysterical symptoms she could not understand. Janet hypnotised her into believing the original traumatic event had never happened and her symptoms disappeared. Marie did not repress her memory, but Janet did it for her. His attitude was – and this also forms part of the range of attitudes in psychotherapy today – that the unfortunate woman had suffered unnecessarily from an earlier trauma and had to disconnect from this aspect of her past to live more fully in the present. The memory was a debilitating encumbrance she was best rid of.

So, when a client of mine insists on treating me with all the expectations derived from the relationship with her mother – who was mean and self-centred – or her father – who had unsatisfied emotional needs and poor sexual boundaries – and constantly projects these expectations onto me and others, it is not a matter of uncovering repression here at all. She remembers what her parents were like and in therapy we can go into her recall of them in detail. The task of memory here is to make the *link* between what she knows of her past and what is happening very much in the present. We are making links between present attitude and past expectations and experience. But we are not only acknowledging the importance of the past in one sense (as the conditions that spawned her expectations of others) but, in another sense, we are also interested in its *irrelevance*. What I mean by this is that, in her present adult life where she is no longer in a dependent relationship to her parents as she was when a child, her expectations, defences and attitudes to people which arose in response to those early relationships are quite out of place. Once recalled in their emotional fullness and relevance, the memories need to be *abandoned* to live a fuller, more authentic emotional life. Not a life being lived as if the same difficulties persisted (leading to her distortion of thoughts and feelings about present relationships) but a life in which these difficulties are clearly perceived as no longer present or evident with those around her. Remembering and forgetting both have their place.

I will return to the specific issue of 'forgotten memories' of childhood abuse later, but now I turn to the second question, what exactly are these memories we refer to anyway? To what extent are they historically true and reliable, and to what extent are they reconstructions? In my client's case it was interesting how the more she 'recalled' of her early life and the more we monitored how she acted as if she were still in that situation, the less black and white would the qualities of emotions become; the less she would either condemn or idealise others but was more able to tolerate ambivalent feelings and to wait before rushing into judgements. Her apparently clear memories and their unambiguous emotional tone became fuzzier as she reconstructed them over time and reflected on them during the course of therapy.

The psychologist Elizabeth Loftus has conducted numerous studies which show the degree to which we reconstruct memories as opposed to retrieving them intact from some sort of store, but she also offers a vivid personal example. For 30 years she had thought that it had been her Aunt Pearl who had discovered her mother drowned in a swimming pool when Elizabeth was 14. But when her uncle told her 30 years later that it had been Elizabeth herself who had found her mother's body, 'the memories began to drift back, slow and unpredictable . . . I could see myself, a thin, dark-haired girl, looking down into the flickering blue-and-white pool. My mother, dressed in her nightgown, is floating face down'.[8] Three days later however, the uncle rings and apologises that he had been wrong. Corroborated by other relatives, it *had* been Aunt Pearl who had found her mother and not Elizabeth after all. Loftus writes:

> When my memory was revealed as a false creation, I experienced a strange yearning for the crisp colours and narrative drive of my invented story-truth. That elaborate but completely fabricated memory comforted me with all its detail and precision, it utter lack of ambiguity . . . at least my memory had a beginning, a middle and an end

> . . . When it was gone, all I had left were a few sombre
> details, a lot of empty spaces, and an aching endless grief.[9]

Memories do not need different information to alter dramatically – time will do the job on its own. On two occasions,
the cognitive psychologist Ulrich Neisser asked 44 students
about when they first heard of the space shuttle *Challenger*
disaster – the first time directly after the event, and then again
two and a half years later. The differences in recall were
dramatic. One student said he first heard when 'I was in my
religion class and some people walked in and started talking
about the [explosion] . . . Then after class I went to my room
and watched the TV programme . . . and I got all the details
from that'. Two and a half years later the same student
recalled a very different version of events: 'When I first
heard about the explosion I was sitting in my freshman dorm
with my roommate and we were watching TV. It came on
in a newsflash and we were both totally shocked . . . I went
upstairs to talk to a friend of mine and then I called my
parents'.[10] Moreover, despite being confronted with their
original account in their own handwriting, the students were
astonished and still insisted that their altered memories were
more accurate and 'real'. This leads us to conclude that the
feeling of certainty that often accompanies recalled memories
may have nothing to do with the accuracy of the recollection
itself but is due to other factors entirely. It could be that the
act of recall itself brings with it a feeling of certainty due
to interpersonal reasons such as not wishing to be seen as
ignorant or foolish (or forgetful!).

This type of study also challenges assumptions that
dramatic, more traumatic experiences are remembered *more*
accurately. In other studies, two groups of subjects were
shown the video-film of a robbery. For one group, the video
showed the robbery with a violent ending while the other
group were shown the tape without the violent ending.
The latter group had the best recall of events which led the
researchers to conclude that the more disturbing an experience, the less likely it is that people will recall the events

accurately. This has important implications for the process of law and its reliance on the statements of witnesses in general, but it should also make us think carefully about the apparent recall of so-called repressed memories of traumatic early experiences which may also lead to accusations in courts of law.

Elizabeth Loftus, who has acted as an expert witness in many such cases, has shown how memories of actual events can not only be recalled quite inaccurately, but also how 'memories' of events that did not happen at all can be easily induced by suggestion. Using the family members of her subjects as confederates in the experiment, Loftus induced several different individuals to believe a memory of a childhood event that had never happened. This was a memory of being lost in a shopping mall or store in their childhood. Again using information derived from other family and friends, and before the truth of the experiment was revealed to participants, Loftus asked the test subjects to rate the accuracy of this false memory against three other childhood memories that were factual. Not only did the subjects rate it highly but, just like Loftus' own 'memory' of finding her drowned mother's body, they were also very willing to embellish the induced memory with several 'recalled' details that the original experimental information (that had been fed to them by the family confederates) *did not contain*.[11]

The serious implications of such a finding have been illustrated by the case of a vulnerable man who was arrested for the ritual abuse of his children. Despite his initial disbelief and his denial of the accusations he became all too ready to agree to new charges and to embellish suggestions of further harm under the pressure of police questioning.[12] Ironically, it was the embellishment of such 'memories' of the crime that, due to their impossibility, led to establishing his innocence and reinforcing the points above. Had the details not been impossible they may well have led to a confirmation of his guilt simply because they carried the weight of recalled memory and thus the (false) assurance of their truth as a 'confession'.

In these cases, the memory of certain events intimately connected to the person 'remembering' them forms a narrative of that person's sense of self and of their own motivations. The issue becomes one of coherence in terms of identity and self-knowledge, rather than the truth of events. The inner voice says, 'If I experienced this [or if I committed this], then this is me. I am that person – the person who had that experience [or who committed those acts]'. The sense of self has to be revised according to the nature of what is being apparently recalled. We identify with our memories. The philosopher Ian Hacking points out how this is something recent in western culture, something he calls 'memoro-politics'.[13] The Delphic injunction 'know thyself' which, I believe, still stands as a central justification for what psychotherapy aims to achieve, is nothing to do with remembering our childhood hurts as such. As Hacking puts it, 'It required that we know our character, our limits, our needs, our propensities for self-deception. It required that we know our souls. Only with the advent of memoro-politics did memory become a surrogate for the soul.'[14]

But our identities and our memories are not only *mental* phenomena: they always exist in reference to the *body*, that is, 'me' too. A famous case is that of Madame I. published by French neurologists Deny and Camus in 1905. I. was a 28-year-old woman and was admitted to the Salpetriere Hospital due to her mental confusion – having been found forgetful and wandering about, and undressing herself in the street. Once her general confusion had passed she was able to articulate what she called her 'general insensibility': 'I'm no longer aware of myself as I used to be. I can no longer feel my arms, my legs, my head and my hair. I have to touch myself constantly to know how I am . . . I cannot find myself. I cannot imagine myself. My insensibility is frightening, as if everything were empty.'[15] She also said how, although she recognised her husband and children when they visited, they did not appear as real as they once were. Neither could she remember or imagine what she had once known well – her parents, the interior of her house, the taste of food, the odour of flowers and the voices of her children: 'Sensations never remain with me, and I can never recall them'.[16]

The doctors reported that Madame I. was perfectly clear-headed and that she 'tries to analyse her problems without wild interpretations or hysterical ideas'.[17] I.'s memory functions themselves were not neurologically impaired, as Israel Rosenfield writes, so the key issue here is how the woman's loss of a sense of her body, which was due to neurological brain damage, and the consequent loss of her sense of being an 'I' seems to have resulted in an accompanying loss of memory and recall. This illustrates how 'there are no memories without a sense of self. Without knowledge of one's own being, one can have no reflections . . . [essentially] *Every recollection refers not only to the remembered event or person or object but to the person who is remembering.*'[18] And that person is a body-person. The body is the frame of reference for the memory.

When the famous physician and writer Oliver Sacks suffered from a paralysed leg he felt it was '*not just a lesion in my muscle, but a lesion in me*'.[19] The loss of sensation gave him an experience that went far beyond what one might expect: 'The leg had vanished, taking its "place" with it . . . Could memory help, where looking forward could not? No! The leg had vanished, taking its "past" away with it! I could no longer remember having a leg. I could no longer remember how I had ever walked and climbed . . . my own leg had vanished "into the blue" . . . I couldn't imagine it returning in any "normal" or physical way, because it had vanished from space and time – vanished, taking its space-and-time with it . . .'.[20] The body is key to memory because, in normal circumstances, it supplies a frame of reference that denotes the sense of I-ness or self.

After such dramatic examples I will round off by returning to two rather different issues which arise from the practice of psychotherapy, but which have interesting applications for memory in human interactions in general. One is a study of what leads to momentary forgetting by patients in the psychotherapy session. Using a cohort of 15 patients whose ages varied from 19 to 39, up to 250 psychotherapy sessions were recorded in which instances of momentary forgetting were observed together with whether the memory was recovered or not at the time. Three factors emerged as significant: one was how, just before the forgetting, patients were cognitively disturbed and unclear about what they were saying and how to say it. Secondly, and more interestingly, it was noticed that just before the memory lapse, patients showed '*a heightened insecure involvement with the therapist*'[21] as evidenced by a judgement of the dialogue and by the fact that more explicit references to the therapist were made before instances of forgetting. In support of this idea, it was particularly noticed that the times when a patient would be more likely to feel insecure about the therapist – beginnings and ends of sessions, and at the beginning of the therapy relationship itself – were indeed the times when there were most momentary forgettings. Thirdly, 'around the moment of forgetting *a specific core relationship theme or conflict is activated* in the context of the relationship with the therapist'.[22] Such themes were found to differ across the patients of course, but were consistent within each individual. For my part I find it interesting how this study points out a significant link between a patient forgetting and aspects of his or her relationship with the therapist. Perhaps a detailed study needs to be conducted in the other direction: *to spot what is remembered and when it is remembered*, to see if there is a similar link. Why and when the therapist forgets or remembers would also be of great interest!

Lastly, both due to Freud's original – then abandoned – formulations of childhood sexual trauma as being the cause of adult psychopathology and the more recent revival of this theory in the recovered memory movement in psychotherapy, any consideration of memory and psychotherapy is not only forced to look at child abuse and its long-term effects, but also to consider why this particular form of trauma formed such an intrinsic part of psychotherapy – its image and its aims – throughout the twentieth century. Although this is just one of many memory themes, I could not finish this chapter on memory without a word or two about the ongoing and widespread discussion of recovered memories of childhood sexual abuse. On the one hand it is a relief that the existence of childhood sexual abuse is now taken seriously. On the other hand, it is distressing to hear of cases where therapists seem to have suggested the existence of past abuse and urged clients to recall such events where no memory of them existed previously. Over the years, I have seen many female clients who tell me how they have been sexually molested by male family members and others. Although these memories were painful to recall or discuss, virtually none of these women had ever forgotten what had happened. The events were available to memory to be dealt with carefully and cautiously as the therapy progressed. True, sometimes more vivid recall would occur, but there was never a question of having *forgotten* these traumatic events entirely so that their recall would constitute brand-new knowledge.

I also recall a male client who wanted to believe there was a discrete event of a traumatic nature in his past that, if recalled, would relieve his disturbing symptoms of unreality, lifelessness and uncertainty. But the childhood history he told me had already revealed a catalogue of repeated abandonment and traumatic separation that seemed quite enough to account for his symptoms. Even if they did exist in some repressed form, any further events he had yet to recall – and I was willing to keep an open mind – would hardly surprise me. They would tend to match – rather than surpass – the seriousness of the abusive quality of adult care throughout his childhood. The Jungian psychologist James Hillman has interpreted the contemporary focus on childhood sexual abuse as our secular culture's version of hell. In the absence of an organised image of heaven and hell, the contemporary psyche still seeks out its horrors and hell gets created anew in the horrors committed against children. But to reduce the aim of psychotherapy to making such a hell its object strikes me as far too narrow a focus.

As I have been saying, memory in psychotherapy involves more than trauma – whether it be repressed, recalled, suggested or discovered. Memory involves the whole person, their body-self and their relationships-self; it involves the past and the recently passed present, as experienced with the therapist and with the rest of the world. Memory is key to self-identity and individuation and deserves deep respect – perhaps not so much as a 'royal road' to psychological health, but as a many-laned highway to the healing of souls. As with poor Christine Beauchamp, being a person means remembering who you are, who you are not, and being happy enough with that. As long as the rest of your world lets you. As we have seen, memory is far from a guarantee of truth, but this is only a problem if we expected it to provide that function in the first place. Memory helps us make the narratives of ourselves coherent and consistent. We need to be flexible and to be doing this in relationship with others, but we will always be making, recalling, recognising and, yes, reorganising those memories. Memory is far from being auxiliary to our human being, it is central to being human.

Notes

1 Loftus, E. and Ketcham, K. (1994) *The Myth of Repressed Memory*. New York: St Martin's Press, p. 3.
2 The name Bourne has been used by Hollywood recently, again in connection with a character who cannot remember who they are, in the film *The Bourne Identity* (2002, dir. Doug Liman).
3 Ellenberger, H.F. ([1970] 1994) *The Discovery of the Unconscious: The History and Evolution of Dynamic Psychiatry*. London: Fontana, p. 135. The Ansel Bourne story and others are reproduced with contemporaneous references in Chapter 3 entitled 'The first dynamic psychiatry (1775–1900)'. Hacking (see below) also details several cases.
4 Prince, M. (1900–1) 'The development and genealogy of the Misses Beauchamp: a preliminary report of a case of multiple personality', *Proceedings of the Society for Psychical Research* (London), 15, pp. 466–83.
5 Ibid., p. 468.
6 Loftus and Ketcham, op. cit., p. 38.
7 Hacking, I. (1995) *Rewriting the Soul: Multiple Personality and the Sciences of Memory*. Princeton, NJ: Princeton University Press, p. 261
8 Loftus, and Ketcham op. cit., p. 39.
9 Ibid., p. 40.
10 Ibid., p. 92.

11 Ibid., pp. 92–100.
12 Crews, F. *et al.* (1997) *The Memory Wars: Freud's Legacy in Dispute.* London: Granta, pp. 187–9.
13 Hacking, op. cit., p. 260.
14 Ibid., p. 260.
15 Rosenfield, I. (1992) *The Strange, Familiar and Forgotten: An Anatomy of Consciousness.* London: Picador, p. 39.
16 Ibid., p. 40.
17 Ibid.
18 Ibid., pp. 41–2.
19 Ibid., p. 51.
20 Ibid., pp. 51–2.
21 Luborsky, L. *et al.* (1979) 'The state conducive to momentary forgetting', in J.F. Kihlstrom and F.J. Evans (eds) *Functional Disorders of Memory.* Hillsdale, NJ: Lawrence Erlbaum Associates, p. 343.
22 Ibid., p. 344.

Snapping and shooting

I had always thought that the famous camera film brand name, Kodak, was a shortened version of some East European name like Kodakily or Kodakoski – either the family name or home town of the inventor. But no. It was the result of George Eastman wanting a brand name that could be pronounced in any language and that would be associated with the sound of a camera. And when you come to think of it, or, rather, say it, 'Koh-dak' *is* a bit like the sound of the shutter going off. A lot more puzzling is the way that photography has coined words used particularly in another field – hunting and ending the lives of animals and birds.

Robin Williams plays the character Cy in the film *One Hour Photo* (2002, dir. Paul Rebenak). He runs a photo-developing service and collects copies of all the photos one family bring in over the years and has them covering a wall of his home. In a sense he has *captured* the family through their images. Photographers talk about *capturing a shot* and when you load video-film clips into a computer editing system like Avid it is also called *capturing* your film clips. Cy tells us that the phrase *snapshot* was originally a term hunters used for a spontaneous shot fired at a fast moving target like a bird or rabbit.

I belong to the internet forum called 'Shooting People' which is for anyone involved in making films. There are at least three meanings to the phrase but we can dismiss the idea that this has anything to do with assassinations or guns. That leaves the double meaning of 'these are people who do shooting – with cameras' and 'this is all about getting images of people down on film'. The similarity between a camera and a gun is the way both have to be pointed in a specific direction towards their target so they can complete their function. While the gun fires a bullet *into* the target, the camera *takes in* light 'firing off' the target. The mechanics seem quite reversed.

But it is the *human intention that is identical*. Both shooters seek to capture something of the other – their target. Both seek to stop the target in time. The hunter stops the prey dead, and the camera stops its prey in just as final a process. But in freezing time onto the tape or frame of celluloid, that moment or moments of life have truly

Figure 8.1 One Hour Photo (Killer Films / The Kobal Collection / Duhamel, Francois)

been *captured*. Something has been *caught*, something of the moment is in the camera now and gone from the target. The target is not dead but in a sense it has had its freedom to flow in time killed. Until the tape or film deteriorates, anyone can now view that single moment, or the actualised moving moments, at any time in the future. No wonder that native peoples were averse to having their photographs taken. Seeing yourself out of time, shot like that, has handed something over to the shooter. You are not dead but the camera-person has captured your image for his or her zoo of souls for ever.

9

Endings, the unconscious and time

A first sign of nascent knowledge is the desire for death.

Franz Kafka

Groundhog Day

So it seems that much of the understanding of our lives as human beings, from the memories we think we have to the meanings that we construct from them, are dependent on our notion of time. In writing about memory in the previous chapter, the concept of time has been taken for granted throughout. Memory and time are two intrinsically connected aspects of how we experience ourselves as human. The conventional view of time divides it into past, present and future, divisions that shift instantly even as you are reading this paragraph. As the poet Wislawa Symborska has put it, 'When I pronounce the word Future, the first syllable already belongs to the past'.

We have been regarding memories as part of the past, but what if we viewed this the other way round? Could it be that our *experience of having memories* is the very thing that *allows the past to exist in our minds*? In other words, memories may not 'come from' the past, but the experience of a memory might be what convinces us there is 'a past' which forms part of something called time that flows in a linear fashion. You may have read the last chapter on memory in the past as it appears to you. In terms of book space, the chapter precedes this one, so you may have skipped it and plan to read it some time in what is 'your' future. Of course, for me, all of this is still in the future as the book has not been published yet and I am at a computer typing these words (26 December 2004, 9.35 p.m. in calendar time) long before your moment of reading them. Whatever the case, in the last chapter I emphasised that memories are a reconstructive process, a creative activity rather than accurate reports of past realities of a present since passed. As such, memories, while appearing to be 'of' the past, always include the 'present' of the time of recall as an unavoidable component of the phenomenon. As the idea of memory becomes less clear, our understanding of time itself follows.[1] So how would it be if time ran differently? What would that do to our human being?

The movie *Groundhog Day* (1993, dir. Harold Ramis), starring Bill Murray, presents its story in the straightforward style of modern Hollywood films, but the conventional narrative is compromised by the way in which it shows the main character, Phil Connors, repeating the same day's events time after time after time. Unlike other movies that repeat one dramatic event with different points of view or time-twists like Kurosawa's *Rashomon* (1980) and *Run Lola Run* (1999, dir. Tom Tykwer), *Groundhog Day* involves a low-key, almost banal repetition of a single day where nothing much happens. Nothing, that is, until Bill Murray's character engages with the fact that he is stuck in repeating time and experiments with his life, his choices and his decisions, knowing he is always destined to wake up and start the same day all over again. Watching this film, we are given an opportunity to see what life might be like with a different experience of time. Bill Murray's character is a TV weather forecaster. Of all the tasks of prediction left in contemporary culture since the demise of oracles, divination and astrology as trustworthy resources, the weather forecaster remains as the one we trust to predict the future – at least as far as the elements are concerned. He or she alone is entrusted with the business of presenting future events in the here and now, several times a day on TV and radio.

Figure 9.1 Groundhog Day (Columbia/Tri-Star/The Kobal Collection)

This particular weather reporter is shown to be an arrogant man and poorly in touch with anything but an ego- and persona-focused way of conducting his life. He is a character heading for a fall. His TV station decide to send him with a small film crew to an upstate country town where the annual celebration of the first day of spring – the eponymous Groundhog Day – is due to take place. They stay the night in a hotel and the next day the filming is completed, but the crew are prevented from returning to the city due to severe weather conditions blocking the roads – an event which had *not* been foreseen! So they have to spend a second night in the hotel and when the weatherman wakes the next morning there is exactly the same record being played on the radio as there was the day before – followed by exactly the same announcement: it is still Groundhog Day. From then on the weatherman is destined to an inexorable cycle of repeated events which none of his ego-based efforts are able to prevent, avoid or alter. Not until, that is, he is able to let his one-sided ego-consciousness, which has become inflated with narrow self-importance, give way to realising the tragic hopelessness of his position. Only at this moment, which is the moment of death for his former personality, does something get reformed. As Jung says, 'It is as though, at the climax of the illness, the destructive powers were converted into healing forces'.[2] In this case, the weatherman's reconnection with the neglected aspects of himself is signalled by his starting to make true connections with other people – beginning with the beggar who he has ignored, repeatedly, up till then.

What can we learn from this story about time? The weatherman and his story remind me of two aspects of psychological suffering and the opportunity offered by psychotherapy. First, we could see him like the person who, through fear, anxiety and insecurity, clings to known habits and obsessions, including a rigid and narrow sense of their own identity. They achieve a form of self-containment, which protects their vulnerability but, like the Uroboros (the image of the serpent in a circle eating its own tail), such a closed circle of containment prevents further inner and outer connections which might ameliorate their position. Secondly, and at the same time, it could be viewed that the Groundhog Day itself, with its own circular Uroboric time that *it imposes* on the weatherman, in fact provides the very opportunity that this soul needs. By preventing him from moving on in time, the endless Groundhog Day forces him to reflect on his own attitude. At the same time, it provides a containment – an endless, timeless opportunity for his soul to comprehend this insight. In this way we can see the similarity between the containing Day and the containment of psychotherapy. Both offer an opportunity for the dominant conscious attitude to be challenged. But both entail suffering – the suffering connected with the first insight into the self and self's possibilities, which are not yet available. Such a moment, which seems like a beginning is, in fact, also an ending – it is the death of the old personality structures. To put it more accurately, it is the beginning of the ending since it does not even allow for giving up. In the film the weatherman commits suicide several times but, of course, wakes up every day in the same hotel room on the same Groundhog Day. Kafka expressed this fear of the Herculean task of addressing the unconscious well: 'A first sign of nascent knowledge is the desire for death. This life seems unendurable, any other unattainable'.[3]

Psychotherapy and time

Despite assertions about how it lay outside the space and time of consciousness, the psychoanalytic conception of the unconscious has relied heavily on analogies and metaphors that involved both space and time. Freud's original formulations made the concept of time implicit in his medical model of psychological healing: the symptom is in time-present, the trauma or cause in time-past, and the cure in time-future. Freud developed this chronological relationship between symptom, cause and cure by coining metaphors derived from the new and exciting sciences of archaeology and geology which, together with evolutionary theory, were redescribing the human present of the mid-nineteenth century in terms of a history of the world longer than that of the prevailing ideas derived from the Old Testament Bible.

Metaphorical images derived from geology and archaeology not only offered Freud the idea of something buried, unfathomable and hidden from consciousness, but also the idea of successive layers or strata through which one *descended*, in the spatial dimension, and *regressed back through*, in the time dimension. Freud was employing this metaphor in *The Aetiology of Hysteria* in 1896 where he compares the psychoanalyst to an explorer coming upon an expanse of ruins in a 'little-known region':

> he may set the inhabitants to work . . . Together with them he may start upon the ruins, clear away the rubbish, and, beginning from the visible remains, uncover what is buried . . . the discoveries are self-explanatory: the ruined walls are part of the ramparts of a palace or a treasure-house . . . the numerous inscriptions . . . when they have been deciphered and translated, yield undreamed-of information about the events of the remote past.[4]

The image is one of the explorer/analyst going to work on the ruins/mind with the help of the inhabitant/patient to 'uncover what is buried'. Significantly, what gets uncovered are not monuments *of* the past but monuments *to the past*, 'the monument that was originally intended to immortalize its historic moment in stone disintegrates into relics or fossils which mutely record the inexorable passage of time'.[5] A link is being made between the concepts of now and then, and the concepts of *disintegration* and *reintegration* and the concepts of *unity* and *separation*.

Jung also employed the metaphor of layers or strata in the unconscious. His image of the phylogenetic (evolutionary) origins of the human psyche meant we all carried within the collective unconscious the developmental history of human consciousness, ancient and modern. Jung reports a dream of his own which enhanced his convictions and offered him empirical evidence at the same time. Jung dreams he is in a house that is 'my house'.[6] He explores the house and finds the upper storey is decorated in the style of the last two centuries while the lower seems to date from the fifteenth or sixteenth century. His interest increases in intensity as he finds an ancient vaulted room down some stone steps in the cellar – he examines the walls and sees they date from Roman times. After lifting a slab in the stone floor, he descends further and finds himself in a low cave cut into the rock: 'Thick dust lay on the floor, and in the dust were scattered bones and broken pottery, like remains of a primitive culture. I discovered two human skulls, obviously very old and half disintegrated. Then I woke up'. For Jung the house represented 'a kind of image of the psyche . . . of my then state of consciousness, with hitherto unconscious additions . . . the long uninhabited ground floor in medieval style, then the Roman cellar, and finally the prehistoric cave. These signified past times and past stages of consciousness'.[7]

Jung's dream about descending through the layers of his house was also a dream about endings and beginnings and, for Freud, about death. When Jung told Freud his dream on board a ship on their way to the USA in 1909, Freud got stuck on the image of the two skulls in the cave at the end of the dream and according to Jung 'returned to them repeatedly, and urged me to find a *wish* in connection with them. What did I think about these skulls? And whose were they? I knew perfectly well . . . what he was driving at: that secret death-wishes were concealed in the dream . . . I felt violent resistance to any such interpretation. I also had some intimation of what the dream might really mean'.[8] This is one of those moments, Freud's fear of Jung's wish to bring him down, that is regarded as an indication of the impending split between the two great founders of depth psychology. And so, ironically, Freud's intuition about a death-wish was not so far off the mark. The different perspectives on the psychological 'past' and the history of consciousness, which Freud and Jung reveal, and the resulting differences in attitude to 'reconstruction' of unconscious contents, contributed to the death of the Freud-Jung collaboration.

But this ending of the relationship was also a beginning – it freed Jung to pursue his path in investigations of the psyche, which were to contrast with the almost exclusively clinical emphases in the development of psychoanalysis. The contrasting images of the personal past of the unconscious expressed in the metaphor of layers of buried material laid down in the historic past, itself led to a death and a rebirth. Jung had asked himself, 'On what premises is Freudian psychology founded? . . . What is the relationship of its almost exclusive personalism to general historical assumptions? My dream was giving me the answer. It obviously pointed to the foundations of cultural history – a history of successive layers of consciousness'.[9]

Romantic time and geological time

The geological and archaeological metaphors would not have been available to Freud or Jung a hundred years beforehand. Around the end of the eighteenth century a shift occurred in the European conception of time partly based on the shift from an agrarian society to the industrial age, partly on the new scientific discoveries, but, just as importantly, also based on a growing romantic and nostalgic reaction to both of these. Don Gifford suggests in *The Farther Shore* that these shifts in the concept of time can be tracked through the literature of that period. Interestingly, the main shift in this period (from 1800 until 1848 or so) seems to be that between Romantic time and geological time. In Romantic time, Europeans were able to find an individual relationship between eternal time and human fast time. One example is Wordsworth's poem 'Tintern Abbey' where his revisiting a scene in the present time is underlined by the way he supplies the reader with the date: 13 July 1798. The poem describes how Wordsworth finds in the beauty of the Wye valley – in its 'organic continuity of landscape, cliffs and sky' – a recognition of something eternal he had been carrying within himself and which the scene helped him recall:

> A motion and a spirit, that impels
> All thinking things, all objects of all thought,
> And rolls through all things.[10]

A sense of the slow time of the eternal and the fast time of humans gets combined again in Keats' 'Ode on a Grecian Urn'. The 'silence and slow time' of the urn's existence across the centuries becomes a metaphor for eternity when compared with the fast time of the human figures depicted in the frieze around it. And although in logic, time and eternity are mutually exclusive, in the poetic (or idealised or Romantic) imagination, the survival of the urn into the fast time of the future invokes the transcendence of time which is eternity.

These views may be compared with Shelley's vision of the two tracks of slow and fast time in the poem 'Mont Blanc: Lines Written in the Vale of Chamouni'.[11] Unlike Wordsworth's confidence in the organic wholeness of himself and the scenery, Shelley, barely 20 years later, envisions the geological source of the mountain and how the 'Power' that made Mont Blanc, 'is not eternally at rest (even though the mountain seems eternal) but forever continuing its process of geological change in a fast-time that seems slow because it is of almost unimaginable duration'.[12] This is the awe-inspiring thing for Shelley, 'which teaches awful doubt'.

The concept of geological time began in the 1780s and 1790s and was to be a source of deep disturbance to generations of Victorians for whom biblical history and the medieval-Renaissance assumptions about the mutual exclusivity of the duration of human time and the duration of eternity were paramount. In 1650, Archbishop Usher had worked out that Creation – i.e. Genesis, Chapter 1, Verse 1 – had begun at 9 a.m. on 26 October 4004 BCE. John Hales, in a different calendarisation, dated Noah's Flood to 5005 years before 1850. The discoveries of geology, followed by the even more challenging ideas of Darwin's evolutionary theories in *On the Origin of Species* in 1859, 'increased the awful doubt that perhaps the universe in its millions of years of slow fast-time was at best indifferent, and at worst positively inimical, to human beings and the few thousand years of their history'.[13]

The Victorian faith in moral and spiritual human progress that would result from the economic and technological progress advancing into the future in the material world gave rise to a compensatory search for 'origins' in the past. Examples of such a nostalgic longing for time past are the search for the site of King Arthur's Camelot in the British Isles or Schliemann's extravagant claims for his discoveries of the real Troy in the Middle East. It is under these conditions – a faith in the progress of mankind in tandem with a backward-looking yearning for the past – that we encounter the beginnings of psychoanalysis. And with it, as we have seen, the concept of an unconscious psyche with its contents buried, fragmented and hidden in a personal past for Freud and layered as the intact farther shores of the mind in the collective unconscious for Jung. This conceptualising of the psyche within the problematic of human fast time and 'eternal' slow time seems to be no coincidence and to be highly relevant. It seems to be a way of addressing the disjunction, the 'awful doubt' brought about by the impact upon European consciousness of a geology and evolution utterly indifferent to human concerns, just when human rationality was at its peak of confidence. The dominant Enlightenment view of human consciousness as expressed by Descartes and Locke had hitherto found the concept of an unconscious illogical. By the end of the nineteenth century, psychoanalysis had restored the unconscious to a central position.

In one way, by introducing the eternal slow time of the unconscious into the human psyche itself, a linking of the human and the eternal could be achieved once more. This would not be without its problems – after all, the 'truth' lying in the strata of geology and the remains of evolution had to be dug up and reassembled in human fast time or, for psychology, in consciousness. We should note how the geological landscape and the psyche seem to hold the past and present together once again in that, for both, the hidden strata exist simultaneously as both *having been* laid down in the past' and *are now* lying down in the present'. So perhaps an important aspect that lies within this project of investigating the buried contents of the unconscious is the restoration of the eternal – that is, the time, or the psyche, which has *no ending or beginning*.

Twentieth-century time: the moment and . . .

Perhaps two of the most distinguishing characteristics of time for us in the twentieth century were the sense of time as a *moment* and time as a *commodity*. I think that both these ways of conceptualising time impact upon human lives and our feelings about beginnings and endings – not to mention what goes on in between.

Let us examine the *moment* first. The mechanised view of the universe developed by the science of the Enlightenment led to the Reverend William Paley's famous metaphor (published in 1802) of 'the universe as a vast watch perfected by God the watchmaker and left to tick away until the God-ordained end of time'.[14] This mechanisation of creation also meant the mechanisation of time and, as Don Gifford argues, 'since time is the medium of memory, the metaphor threatens the mechanisation of memory'.[15] I think this is seldom more evident for us than in the *photograph* – the invention that not only 'sealed down' the understanding of time as a succession of frozen moments, but has now come to dominate the images that constitute our daily lives. Photographs, as much as any other contribution they make to our conscious cognitive and emotional life, persuade us towards the view that time consists of a series of 'moments'. The photograph stands as a 'snapshot' of time that freezes one of these moments forever. It seems to represent the technical accomplishment of 'stopping time' or at least of providing a recording, apparently, of one of time's 'moments'. This image of time appeals to our modern consciousness that is forever fragmenting the world of experience into more manageable portions for us to understand and manipulate more easily.[16]

From its inception, the photograph provided the illusion that a moment of the present could be grasped and frozen so that the moment would be available in the future and – apart from its unreliable recall through the medium of memory – not lost forever. Through the technology of a shutter clicking open briefly to allow light to fall on a sensitised plate, the photograph in fact *created the concept of the moment*, as if all experienced time was merely and always a succession of these moments, as brief as you could imagine. In doing so, it probably contributed to that very sense of the unreliability of our memory. A photograph, it was once thought, was the gold standard for verifying an event.

When it comes to the moving photographic image, this was originally no more complicated than a series of these snapped moments streaming past a projectionist's light and past our visual field, nowadays at 24 frames per second. But, asks Jungian analyst Pat Berry,[17] what was the attraction of this technology to the late nineteenth-century urban individual who flocked, as one of thousands, to watch the Lumiere brothers' short films of *Workers Leaving the Factory* and *Feeding the Baby* in the basement of a Paris café in the late 1890s?[18] She connects this fascination with the speeding up of urban life – a time of overwhelming acceleration and confusion of human experience, which began around the 1850s and which has increased exponentially ever since. Berry's point is that photography and the moving image offered the population a way of savouring the present – emotionally, cognitively and reflectively – in times when daily conscious perception was becoming overwhelmed, confused and in need of adjustment. The photographic recording and framing of moments of time comforted the psyche of the modern citizen while convincing the population even further that time really *was* consisting of moments either captured or being ceaselessly tipped into the past. Of course this coincided with the whole emotional, rational and economic idea of human *progress*. This was the need to emphasise a *present with an eye on the future far more than the past* – an idea and an attitude initiated in the late Enlightenment and raised to its highest glory in the Victorian era.

At the same time (the beginning of the twentieth century) the psychologist William James was already questioning the concept of the 'moment of time'. He came to the conclusion that the present moment was not so much a 'knife-edge' but more a 'saddleback, with a certain breadth of its own on which we sit perched and from which we look in two directions into time'.[19] Don Gifford takes this revision and

Figure 9.2 Mother and Child

applies it to the photograph by pointing out how the snap-shot (like the one above, Figure 9.2) is 'Not a point in time at all but a locus or duration block that includes overlapping phases in the times of several lives – the child's and the photographer's and the anonymous darkroom drudge's who made the print and the mother's'.[20]

It is the metaphor of the mechanisation of time that per-suades us of the fine exactitude of a moment in time that the photograph has supposedly captured. I think we can push this metaphor back on itself for our purposes here. Picture this! What if we step back for a moment and regard our everyday consciousness as equivalent to the photograph. Or, more accurately, let us liken the activity of our conscious mind to an endless sequence of photographs – like the images flowing at 24 frames per second, which produce the illusion of the movie picture. This is *Kairos* – the cleverness of con-scious time. But the ground of all this, *the rich unfrozen movement from which all these 'still' frames derive, is the uncon-scious.* The unconscious can be likened to the other 'real' life being lived outside and beyond the lens of consciousness, sometimes coinciding, but ultimately independent of it.

. . . the commodity

Time is also a *commodity*. It has become a measure of work and of value. Although we are paying a bricklayer to lay 100 bricks, the fact that we estimate him to lay 50 bricks in one hour leads us to pay him 'by the hour'. Clock time is an analogy of work done, but we treat it much more like an equivalence. In Jonathan Swift's *Gulliver's Travels*, the Lilliputians think that Gulliver's watch must be his god as he seems to consult it whenever he is about to do anything. Similarly, there is something godlike about the way clock time governs our work activities from serving in a shop to working as a lawyer, or as a psychotherapist or a plumber.

Gulliver was one of our era's earliest mechanised men, but when travel was by foot or by horse, time and space seemed to be in harmony with the human scale, with human needs and human expectations. On foot or on horseback the focus of visual perception is either on the roadside or on a few yards ahead. With the speed of the train, and later the car, these are rendered a blur and so the focus is forced upon some distance ahead and on the horizon itself as these are the only views that are still moving at a pace that the eye can take in and accommodate. The nineteenth-century French painter Henri Matisse insisted on being driven at no more than five kilometres per hour, 'otherwise you have no sense of the trees'. Incidentally, this point gets made in the recent movie of *Dr Doolittle* (1998, dir. Betty Thomas) played by Eddie Murphy, where he is driving with a talking dog who complains that at this speed he is bored because all he can see are the road markings which compel him to utter: 'line, line, line, line'. Dr Doolittle tells him to look up at the side of the road and watch something more interesting; the dog then says: 'Tree, tree, tree, tree'.

It was around 1760 that Europeans devised a portable chronometer that was reliable enough for fixing one's place by relating to the sun. New inventions like the railway and the telegraph with their speeded up communications demanded a further *standardisation of time*. Time became an aspect of life that needed to be reined in, brought under control for the sake of a rationally organised economic life. The speed of trains gave rise to new timetabling difficulties because if you set your clock at the sun's zenith at 'noon' in London and then travelled to Bristol, you would encounter several clock times along the way (all set by the local reading of the sun's zenith at noon) and a different clock time from your own at your final destination. In the USA the various railroads used to take their times and scheduling from their terminal cities, but when these lines met up in another city (like Cincinnati for example) 'they wound up trying to tell time by as many as five different clocks, varying by as much as 1½ to 2 hours'.[21] This of course led to the standardisation of time – the USA taking up Greenwich Mean Time in 1883 and the rest of the world, bit by bit, doing so by 1904. Airline travel has now led to the structuring of our human-time reality into zones whereby we agree to flick our watches forward or back an hour as we pass through them.

Although there is something very real – and also symbolic – in the way that nature can still intrude, as when she stops our trains with 'leaves on the line' or 'the wrong kind of snow',[22] human labour has now become entirely clock dependent. As Don Gifford puts it, 'Time, measured by the factory clock and whistle [and, I would add, the therapist's watch] relinquishes its bio-logic, and becomes the coinage, money for worker and employer alike, whether the relation is determined by daily or hourly wage or by piecework'.[23]

Even a humane activity like psychotherapy is dominated by the clock-time system. The 'time' of the therapy session is guided and contoured not by anything inherent in the work, let alone inherent in the individual we have with us, but by the social boundaries of time designed to optimise the benefits and profits of a capitalist form of economic behaviour. Rather like what has been achieved in factory farming, psychotherapeutic treatment, inasmuch as it is a commoditised work governed by clock time, feels itself free to more or less ignore the 'seasons' of its own portion of 'nature' – the unconscious. Of course therapists cannot ignore the unconscious and pay it close attention, but they do carry on their practice in a *form* which, in its mechanised way, acts against this type of time.

Although therapists' work has much in common with that of shaman, priests and healers of other times and other places, unlike them, therapists are not directly supported by their community – like other wage labourers, they have to support themselves. But so do their clients, which is how they both come to the agreement on time that they do. In addition there are the constraints imposed on this particular work by the dominant attitude to time elsewhere in the culture. Therapists and clients are both required to share the same need for 'time off', 'time out', 'breaks' and holidays – concepts of time portions all defined as *absences of the work-time routine*. Perhaps the separation-attachment issues that arise in psychotherapy work at these times are as much a protest from the unconscious, where there is no commoditised time, as anything to do with infant fears being relived in the transference as the theories would have it. Rather than a 'vulnerable child', maybe it is *the other time of the unconscious which feels cruelly treated* when required to conform to the clock time of modern consciousness. And the two perspectives are not so separate when we consider how, after all, mothers in the past also had to live in the commoditised time of their adult work and chores, which interrupted their children's play, that could have gone on for eternity. The benefit of clock time as used in industrial production is an apparent freedom of 'choice' when compared with agricultural time where we follow nature and her requirements. But in achieving this apparent freedom of 'choice', we become alienated from the rhythms of nature – and hence from our own inner 'nature', our unconscious inner worlds. Although we cannot get away from it, there is something about the commodified time of psychotherapy that may be working against what the unconscious requires. We can help this, I believe, by paying attention to what we have consciously done with time and remembering the otherness of the unconscious in this respect.

Penultimate conclusion: examples from psychotherapy work

I want to bring my argument into focus on the practical issues and feelings that arise around beginnings and endings in psychotherapy and offer some examples that can be generalised to other human activities. I will be referring to some of the ideas I have set up already – death and rebirth, separation and attachment, the geological metaphor and the loss of eternity, the fiction of the 'moment' and of commodified time, and our inner and outer nature.

It is often troubling to therapists when a client ends their therapy before sufficient work has been done or change has been achieved. I had such a client who left after six months and who I did not see again for four years. Then she contacted me again and I saw her for six months once more and, once again, she talked about leaving. She was quite a depressed person and did not believe there was any good to be found in herself that was worth devoting therapy time and money to. She had been prompted to return to me because she thought her 'time was up' – she had a breast tumour but it turned out to be benign. But she felt it was now 'too late' for therapy, she felt she had failed to achieve any of her potential in life and did not want to continue feeling this in the context of a psychotherapy that would be a constant reminder of her stuckness. She was one of those clients who make me feel particularly stupid and inadequate. Everything I had to say seemed naive and inconsequential – just words. This was nothing to do with her, or my own conscious abilities, but more because I did not feel I could speak to her depths – so I could not speak 'in depth' and I felt shallow. Within this person I sensed a wide gulf between the conscious and the unconscious. The unconscious informing and nurturing ground of her personality – the self in Jungian terms – was, for her, far out of reach. Of course, this had implications for her relationship with the personal and archetypal mother and what it meant to be a woman in general. But what concerns us here is the way that her 'basic fault' (and Balint who coined this phrase about the source of some mental health difficulties meant this in a geological not a moral sense) had left her cut off not only from the ground of the unconscious but also the ground of eternal time, or unconscious time. For her the sessions were dominated by conscious time and its moments. The commodified time of the psychotherapy session and its cost was also a dominant concern. Although she could well afford the therapy, and was given some money she was to use for it, she often brought up the *value* of the therapy to her in financial terms. She was not yet able to start to connect with the unconscious time of therapy where the work happens. She was primarily aware of her conscious time with me, and in her pain and depression, she wanted it to end.

Another example is a psychotherapy case where, quite unusually, I ended the work with the client myself after two and a half years. This woman began therapy with a good motivation, but she actually never began at all. By this I mean that she never began to engage with her unconscious psyche. Her dreams and the quality of the relationship with me remained very static and stereotyped from the beginning – despite the way she seemed keen to come and was able to express her distress and unhappiness with what we call 'appropriate affect'. When I began to wonder about her lack of real engagement in the therapy, after a period of her complaining about the lack of progress in herself and in her life, she revealed her attitude with this statement: 'Well it's like the monkey and the typewriter. If you put a monkey in front of a typewriter and give him long enough he'll write Shakespeare. So I just keep coming and hope for the best.' On reflection, I don't know whether it was she or myself who was meant to be the monkey working so randomly and in the dark, but this self-image and other factors persuaded me that I was not the right therapist for this person. The image seemed so detached from any sense of her own human being and her own potential for self-healing. In its emptiness and randomness, the image of the monkey at the typewriter suggested a poor link with her unconscious inner world and a lack of hope which could stem from its 'other' eternal time. In the image of herself as the monkey at the typewriter, the eternal becomes 'given enough time' – the eternal is replaced by lots and lots of clock time as if this were an equivalent, when it is completely missing the point. The image and the psychological position this patient reveals is that of an over-conscious attitude or orientation that is quite out of touch with its unconscious source.

It seems to me that the degree to which a client is over-concerned with 'moments' – the need for 'aha!' realisations or something 'happening' every session – or is over-concerned with the 'commodity' of the session – is a good indicator of the degree of disconnection between the ego and the self which lies behind their suffering. I have another client who illustrates this concern with moments by often saying 'I don't know where to go with this' or 'It seems a bit of a waste of time here today'. It is hard for him to feel that *anything* is proceeding unless he is consciously aware of it in the succeeding 'moments' of the session. The clients who have less of a problem with the regular slow pace of the psychotherapy sessions are often more at ease either because some healing work has helped the ego-self-relationship already, or because this split was never their particular problem in the first place. They attend regularly and seldom complain about the session on the local scale but tend to view the work as integrated into a longer overall period of their lives which bears a closer relationship to daily life outside, while also meaning something else, and something more, within them. When such patients look back at the number of years they have been coming, the years do not feel like the same sort of years with which they would measure other events in their lives. Their experience seems to be one of a quite different time – unconscious time, emotional time, whatever it is called – that they accept as persisting *alongside* daily clock and calendar time. Interestingly, in these clients, this attitude coincides with their making far less of a connection between the session and its financial cost. For them, the whole project of working with and within one's unconscious in psychotherapy becomes much more a process of *life*, integrated within the personality as it unfolds and grows, and not a 'measurable' or economically determined entity on its own.

Ultimate conclusion: making the best use of the (concept of) time

So let me begin my ending of this reflection on time. I have not forgotten Bill Murray as the poor weatherman I mentioned at the start – locked in his Uroborically repeating Groundhog Day. Trapped in his one-sided ego/persona he lives an endless cycle of birth and death rather like the Buddhists' *samsara* – our daily life of illusion which is out of touch with the absolute. The weatherman is out of touch with the unconscious and thus the rest of his personality and his human being. It seems that his experience of an endless repetition of time and the absence of any endings and beginnings has been necessary in order for him to connect with his soul. But even in its absence here, let us not get seduced by the 'effects' of linear time. *Just as neurotic suffering is not the beginning of therapy, neither is transformation the end*. Equally, neither is *no transformation* a premature ending or unfinished work. If the life of the unconscious is truly the ground of our being, as I believe it is, our true human being – *life itself* – then time and its punctuations as understood by the conscious mind is quite secondary and need not be regarded as determining.

If we are able to regard psychotherapy and the individuation it promotes as a flow between death and rebirth, between integrations and deconstructions, between attachments and separations, then there are only 'sort of' endings and beginnings for psyche. And similarly, the cycle of the seasons in nature consists of only a 'sort of' death and rebirth – in the *whole pattern* of the seasons there are actually no such 'moments' of chopped up time. Who can say when winter ends and spring begins? These are merely two of our human 'time words' that we use for convenience. In nature they are hardly relevant. It may be truer to say that, as in outer nature, the inner nature of the psyche holds a similar tendency – the tendency for each ending or beginning to be making way for its other. The consciously perceived, registered and decided-upon 'endings' in the 'time' of therapy have an unconscious dimension that is *forever out of time and equivalent to the eternal*.

How could the work of psychotherapy possibly be effective unless the unconscious 'session' never really ended between sessions? It is not even memory that is the concern here. Conscious memory is as mechanised and chopped up – as well as stratified for Freud and Jung – as the clock time or calendar it is often judged by. No, it is the forging and strengthening of an unconscious connection that our human being aims at and which does the healing. Only in this way is time a healer. This time can be viewed as an archetype that structures our experience. In this way we can repossess it as a psychic possession of our own, deriving from the unconscious and rendered in consciousness in consistent images and experiences according to the local cultural and historical circumstances. Thus we may avoid time being experienced as alien and outside of ourselves or making us its victim. We may avoid making every day Groundhog Day.

Notes

1 That's OK, go ahead and see how many pages are left in this book. At some point, your first reading of it will, like everything else, be a 'thing of the past'.

2 Jung, C.G. (1932) 'Psychotherapists or the clergy', in *The Collected Works*, Vol 11 (1969). London: Routledge & Kegan Paul, para. 534.

3 Kafka, F. (1970) 'Reflections on sin, pain, hope and the true way', in

The Great Wall of China: Stories and Reflections. New York: Schocken Books. p. 164.

4 Freud quoted in Reinhard, K. (1996) 'The Freudian things: construction and the archaeological metaphor', in Barker, S. (ed.), *Excavations and their Objects: Freud's Collection of Antiquity.* Albany, NY: State University of New York Press, p. 60.

5 Reinhard, ibid.

6 Jung C.G. (1967) *Memories Dreams, Reflections.* London: Flamingo, p. 183.

7 Ibid.

8 Ibid.

9 Ibid., p. 185.

10 Wordsworth quoted in Gifford, D. (1990) *The Farther Shore: A Natural History of Perception 1798–1984.* London: Faber & Faber.

11 Shelley, P. (1816) quoted in Gifford, ibid.

12 Gifford, ibid., p. 83.

13 Ibid., p. 85.

14 Ibid., p. 73.

15 Ibid.

16 Psychotherapists' conscious experiences with their patients are also understood within this paradigm. Each session has a beginning and an ending and the dialogue in between is assumed to be able to flow in a linear fashion whereby, at the end of the 'hour', some understanding, or knowledge or aspect of relationship, may be experienced that was not experienced or known at the 'beginning' of the hour. But as we all know, therapy sessions do not necessarily proceed in such a way. The therapeutic encounter is a time set apart from linear conscious experience which allows for the unconscious to emerge in its own way. This is a way that need not follow our dominant conscious experience of moments in time flowing in a linear sequence from past to present like a train passing through an 'unknown' landscape gradually making it 'known' as time moves on. And if this paradigm of conscious time is not true of the unconscious on the micro-scale of the individual session, what are we to make of our assumptions about the patient who ends 'too soon'? And, on the grandest scale, what about the apparent stages of libidinal and ego 'development' which are theorised as following a linear path from the oral to the anal to the genital. And further, what of the sequence child to adolescent to adult? These categories in our present consciousness – such as 'infancy', 'childhood', 'adolescence', 'maturity' – have not necessarily existed in other times and other cultures; and even less so have the Freud/Abraham libidinal 'stages' I just mentioned. The 'time' of the unconscious may, in reality, have no resemblance to the time we 'experience' from time to time. Even birth and death, the ultimate 'moments' in consciousness, may be quite

different for the unconscious. Perhaps the research on so-called near-death experiences is evidence for this.

17 Berry, P. (2001) 'Image in motion', in Hauke, C. and Alister, I. (eds) *Jung and Film: Post-Jungian Takes on the Moving Image*. Hove: Brunner-Routledge.

18 This was happening everywhere, not only in France. In 1997, 28 hours of film footage were found by builders in a shop they were renovating in a town in the North of England. This was film shot by Mitchell and Kenyon between 1900 and 1913 of local people, local towns and events and was clearly pursued as an activity thoroughly welcomed by the population who would swarm to the screenings to see themselves as a moving image. The footage was in very good condition and by the time you read this it should be available on DVD.

19 William James quoted in Gifford, op. cit., p. 102.

20 Gifford, ibid., p. 103.

21 While the USA has four time zones, China, surprisingly, has opted for a single time zone. If there was more time I would have liked to ponder the implications of this.

22 These are actual excuses or explanations the rail companies have included in their apologies for train delays in the UK.

23 Gifford, op. cit., p. 97.

The rise of revulsion: spitting and The Stones

In 1964, The Rolling Stones' fourth UK single, 'It's All Over Now' went to number one. While Brian Epstein managed the Beatles' presentation as smart young men in suits and ties, The Stones' manager, Andrew Oldham, inverted the image and supplied the press with slogans like, 'Would you let your daughter go out with a Rolling Stone?' Such was the Stones' image as objects of revulsion – ugly, effeminate, heterosexually rampant and antisocial all at once – at a gig in Blackpool they were spat at by males angry that their girlfriends were attracted to the group.[1] On their early visits to the USA The Stones were spat at by waiters, passers-by, drivers and, well, anyone within spitting distance. Spitting has long been a way of expressing social disapproval and showing the spittee, as I suppose you'd call them, a vehement hatred and disdain.

Fast forward to 1976 and we find the audience spitting at bands again – this time their targets are The Sex Pistols and The Clash and all the other groups in the first wave of the new punk rock. But wait, something has changed. The band members still look revolting, check, the press is full of condemning publicity, check, the establishment is up in arms once more, check, but who is doing the spitting? It is the *fans*! In 1976 spitting was a sign of appreciation of your band, a gob of approval flung at the musicians between swigs of lager and sniffs of amphetamine sulphate. Punk sought to recreate the raw energy of early rock music like The Stones, because the feeling was that by 1976 such groups had become rock dinosaurs, rich and lazy, out of touch with the fans. Along with the rudimentary musicianship, disapproval of parents and scruffy clothing, came the spitting of the audience. The picture was complete. An image of the 'original' rebellious, raw, energetic British rock was back on the scene. But, far from being an authentic revival, punk rock was a thin *simulacra* – meaning it was a representation of something that had never really existed. And what gives it away? The spitting of course. In 1964 the spitting defined a hatred and rejection of what The Stones stood for and represented. We know this because the ones who spat at them were not fans but people who *hated* the group,

Figure 9.3 Gimme Shelter (Maysles/Maysles/20th Century Fox / The Kobal Collection)

their music and everything they thought they stood for. In 1976, the kids who *loved* The Sex Pistols showered them with spittle to show their love and appreciation. Take a snapshot of people spitting at either The Stones or The Pistols and it might *look* the same. But the second time the real spitting was over. The greatest signifier of disapproval got revived but with a mirror-image meaning – appreciation and approval. When such a thing happens, the days are numbered for the hope that popular youth music might offer an authentic challenge to the dominant culture. As the song goes, 'It's all over now'.

Note

1 Bockris, V. (1993) *Keith Richards: The Biography.* London: Penguin, p. 72.

10

Orpheus, Dionysus and popular culture: Jean Cocteau's *Orphee* – then and now

> Silence goes faster when it goes backwards.
> A single glass of water lights the world.
> <div align="right">The radio in <i>Orphee</i> (Cocteau, 1950)</div>

It has been said of contemporary films like *American Beauty* (1999, dir. Sam Mendes), for example, that they are 'a lightning conductor . . . [or] a vessel into which people can pour their anxieties and fantasies'.[1] 'Watching dreadful things in the movies', says Christopher Frayling, 'helps one come to terms with them in everyday life . . . the first horror movie was in the Lascaux caves thirty-two thousand years ago'.[2] And, just as those artists represented the creatures they hunted and killed as a way of coming to terms with their fear of them, it is significant to note how in the two months after the attack on the Twin Towers in Manhattan, there was a 50 per cent rise in rentals of disaster movies from the Blockbuster stores.

But what of the significance of films from earlier times? How do some movies revive meanings or uncover a new relevance for audiences generations apart? When I began writing this piece in March 2004, Cocteau's 1950 film *Orphee* was being shown in London in a brand new print. In the *London Evening Standard* that week the film ranked number

Figure 10.1 Orphee (Andre Paulve/Films Du Palais Royal/The Kobal Collection)

one in their list of must-see screenings competing with new releases like *Cold Mountain*. How come? Why this contemporary interest in a movie which is now 54 years old – younger than Mick Jagger but older than rock 'n' roll? And why now, at this moment?

It is the way in which my unconscious threw up that – seemingly random – link to the singer and songwriter for The Rolling Stones that has given me a clue. It is the combination of the Orpheus of myth – lyric poet, troubadour for the

Argonauts, inspiration for some, a rebel sacrificed by others – and the poet as youth icon in Cocteau's movie, that has directed me towards a new significance of Orpheus for contemporary times. Of course, this is not *new* at all, but, by refreshing Orpheus on the screen we refresh our view of the character and the myth, we revitalise it and bring out, maybe not *new*, but certainly *fresh* meaning. Our era is one that adores novelty; newness can sometimes override the content of a long familiar image or meaning and make us open to it once again. In our times maybe this virtual novelty is just what we need to recognise an image that has been worn out by knowing it too long. Maybe the not-new 'newness' can override our sense of thinking we 'knew' all about Orpheus already.

In Cocteau's retelling of Orpheus' story, it is the competition between the old and the new, imposed and enacted by the youthful crowd using the 'old' poet – Orpheus – and the new upstart poet Cegeste, that underpins the myth's relevance for an audience in 1950. In the opening scenes, Orpheus and Cegeste, surrounded by a crowd of young men and women, look like Frank Sinatra and Johnny Halliday *personae*: early 'youth icons' who Cocteau uses to embody and signify the break – in France – between the generation that suffered Nazi occupation and the post-war generation just six years later. We are only looking at a ten-year age difference between the two poets – but this is at the start of an era which witnessed the beginning of rock 'n' roll and the invention of the 'teenager' which saw *youth* fly up the charts of all that was best about life. An examination of this moment should help us understand why Orpheus was on our minds again in 2004 – both as a theme for the journal Spring and as a film-screening in London. Just after the credits, at the start of Cocteau's film, a voice tells us:

> We chose the legend of Orpheus . . . the gifted minstrel Orpheus could even charm wild animals. But his songs estranged him from his beloved wife Eurydice – and Death took her away from him. Orpheus entered the Underworld, where he charmed

Death into allowing Eurydice's return to the world of the living on the condition that he should never again look upon her. However, he did and was then destroyed by the Maenads. Where, and in what century does the tale unfold? Legends are timeless, it is their privilege. Let us begin –

This leads us to expect a rather uncomplicated retelling, then, promising nothing radical perhaps, except for two small pointers: *'We chose'* this legend, and, *'Where, and in what century does the tale unfold?'* both of which I take as Jean Cocteau having something to say about what was happening in 1950 that the myth speaks to. With the hindsight of 54 years, years where established ideas have been challenged by the young and popular culture forms, like cinema and rock music, have claimed a place beside establishment arts – Cocteau's re-spinning of the Orpheus story seems spot on. Cocteau sets his story of Orpheus in his own present place and time, France in 1950. It begins at a café crowded with young people, lively and full of energy and enthusiasm. It's a sort of *Expresso Bongo* or *The Girl Can't Help It* – but more 'Art House' than 'Hollywood' or 'Elstree'. There is an implicit – but not expressed – sense of France five years after World War II: freed from Nazi occupation, its young people bursting with a pent-up zest for life. Or, more accurately, a *renewal of life*: the restoration of lives truncated, held in abeyance, constricted or even curtailed by the political events which began in 1939. Orpheus was the grandson of the goddess of Memory, and at the end of his story, according to tradition, he gets torn apart, dismembered by the Maenads. Cocteau's film begins where people are putting their fragmented lives back together: they are remembering themselves,[3] remembering what it is like to be spontaneous, enthusiastic and Dionysian – dare we say. Relishing life again after the austerity of the preceding years. It is poignantly informative of this threshold moment how a study by the University of Wisconsin in 1950, 'confirmed that the young people of America were "a generation with strongly middle-aged values".'[4]

Orpheus is there with the young people in the café, but he appears slightly older than the rest and less in fashion now. Maybe his time as poet and cult leader has passed as a new young poet – Cegeste, only 18 years old – is around to take his place. Orpheus sits apart and talks to an older teacher – who 'gave up writing twenty years ago' – and is shown a new literary review called Nudisme. *Orpheus opens it and all the pages are blank.*[5]

This reminds me of the scene in the movie *Pleasantville*[6] where in another café, this time in Smalltown USA in the 1950s, the young people of the idealised, black and white, 'Peyton Place' TV town of Pleasantville look at their library books which are similarly blank inside, while they, like the café crowd here, blithely drink their Cokes as if nothing is strange. Bland simplicity and uncomplicated living – implying an immaturity in the face of life's complexity – are present in both cases. While in *Pleasantville* there is a sexless, harmless hedonism, in Cocteau's café there is a caffeine- and alcohol-fuelled, potentially violent hedonism heading for the Dionysian. It is against this youthful, inexperienced and volatile background, which says much about how he has located himself, that we see Orpheus begin his journey.

Back in the film Orphee, *the older man refers to the pages and quips that blank ones are 'less ridiculous' than pages filled with bad poetry. This conversation is referring to the new young poet Cegeste who has now arrived, drunkenly celebrating his success, exciting the girls and causing trouble with the boys like a young Elvis, Jagger or Jim Morrison. A fight starts, the police arrive, and Cegeste resists arrest by biting a policeman; but then two motorcyclists zoom by and knock him down in a hit-and-run. On hand is the woman and her chauffeur who brought Cegeste to the café and now they scoop him up into their Rolls-Royce limousine. The woman orders Orpheus into the car with them because, she says ominously, 'I need you as witness.'*

This is where I think Orpheus begins to resonate so well for us – and resonated so well for Cocteau in the 1950s and, indeed, up until he died. Orpheus is needed as a witness to his own life and death and the life and death of poetry in our postmodern culture. Since the 1940s and 50s and through the following decades – where the term 'the Sixties' constellates what is signified beyond any actual chronology[7] – it's been a case of 'It's poetry Jim, but not as we know it'. Here I am thinking of the earnest attention university academics paid to pop culture from doctorates on Dylan's lyrics and Beatles' songs, through to Madonna's 'function' in feminist culture. There is an adolescent feel to Cocteau's Orpheus, a sense of the *puer* or boy-man and his resistance to growing up despite the arrival of the new young poet Cegeste which suggests that it is time for Orpheus to move on and confront life in a different way. From this perspective, the myth supplies a relevance reborn for an audience at the start of the post-war period – when adolescence was reinvented as the 'teenager', challenging the prevailing 'mature', 'adult' values of European and American culture in particular. From the Beats and beatniks of the late 1940s and 50s, to the pop and rock music of The Beatles, The Rolling Stones, The Doors and others, not to mention gatherings like Woodstock, Altamont, Grosvenor Square, Kent State University, Ohio, and Glastonbury, the soundtrack arose from the poetry of troubadours. The obvious ones were Bob Dylan, Mick Jagger and John Lennon, but Martin Luther King's 'I have a dream' was as lyrical as it comes and some might say carried more clout than any number of refrains of 'We shall overcome'. Even later approaches – in the 1970s – to the just-finished war in Vietnam were brim-full of lyric poetry, as we hear not only in the music soundtrack to Francis Ford Coppola's *Apocalypse Now*, but also in scripted lines like 'I love the smell of Napalm in the morning' and 'Charlie don't surf'. None of this would have been possible without the young, Orphic poetic voices of the era. Just for comparison, check out an old war film like *The Guns of Navarone* for its contrasting, earnest, 'mature' and 'adult' approach to the seriousness of war and heroism.

What is being stirred up goes two ways. On the one hand, there is a regressive *senex*, conservative-father demand to grow up and out of adolescence – to face life's responsibilities and let the next poetic generation take over. As Dustin Hoffman was told at his young character's 'maturation' party in *The Graduate* (1967, dir. Mike Nichols), 'I have one word for you, Benjamin: *plastics!*'. On the other hand, 'anti-maturity' *puer* messages were being flagged up in popular culture by those who rejected being 'grown-up' because it ran the risk of diluting a fantastic new energy found in celebrating the hope, novelty, rebellion and rebirth of new era that seemed synonymous with staying young. Everyone in the early 1950s understood what the hero of *The Catcher in the Rye*,[8] Holden Caulfield – a youngster only permitted a critical voice at the price of a mental breakdown – meant by 'phoney' in reference to everything the American dream had delivered. In the 1960s the straights who did weird stuff like run businesses, have professions, or factory jobs and family lives (usually as parents of their accusers) were called 'plastic people'. Young ideas meant poetic ideas, ideas that were sung more often than written; idealistic expression meant poetic expression, in poetry, music and songs; the rationality of the straights (squares, rubes, whatever) was being side-swiped not by further rational argument but by a far more lyrical and subversive *poetic* 'argument'.

> *In the car, it becomes clear the boy poet Cegeste is dead and the woman tells Orpheus to shut up when he asks about going to a hospital; we strongly get the idea she is something to do with Death. They come to a railway crossing and enter another territory. They have crossed the Styx and the woman tells the driver to 'Take the usual route'. Outside the moving car, the back-projected scenery turns negative. The radio announces surreal lines which Bob Dylan[9] would have been proud of:*

> *'Silence goes faster when it goes backwards . . . three times*
> *A single glass of water lights the world . . . two times'*

The car is joined on the road by the same two black leather-clad, hit-and-run bikers as outriders. Orpheus is openly perplexed and the woman tells him not to be so stupid. She is totally in charge of this situation; Orpheus is along for the ride but, as the contradictions mount up, he is losing track of where this journey is heading.

There is nothing more maturing than the prospect of one's own death, and this is now what confronts Orpheus. (As if that was not maturing enough, later, as we know, he is confronted with the responsibility for his wife Eurydice's life and death as well.) This point is made with further irony by the way in which (at first) it is the new young poet, Cegeste, not the 'has-been' Orpheus, who is dead – allowing Orpheus to meditate, vicariously for the time being, on his own inevitable demise. He is offered the significance of death so he may apply it to his life, but will he take up this chance? And for 'us' in the 1950s audience and in the 2004 audience – what are we to make of these pairs: death of the young poet, coming death of the older poet; death of one, living of the other; the older learning from death of the younger so he may restore his own 'young poet'? We seem to be directed towards a meditation on the renewal of poetry in the culture – the lyrical word revalued and made available for life, for all of us and not as 'art' merely reserved for the few. This strikes me as the birth, or rebirth, of the popular. Come to think of it, this is exactly the significance that the Dionysian attitude (popularly) restored to the population in ancient and recent times. What challenge could be more fitting for a civilisation wracked by the fathers' war fought with Apollonian justification, than the challenge and rebirth that arises from the intoxicated enthusiasm of a Dionysian renewal carried by the ecstatic irrationality of song and dance?

The boy's body is taken into a house by the bikers. This is not quite Hades but it is a House of Death. It was once grand, and is now run-down: we are being invited to look at something that has seen better days. The death of what? Maybe so many

of the values in 'civilised' art and life that were held up to 1949?
As they all go upstairs, the woman asks Orpheus 'Are you
asleep?' He says he thinks so. In a bedroom, she still bosses
him around, he changes the music on the radio, she tells him
off. The radio says 'The mirror would do well to reflect more'
as we see both of them in the mirror. She's a bossy Mrs
Robinson, and Orpheus doesn't know it yet but soon enough
he'll be saying 'I think you are trying to seduce me Mrs . . . ?'
A pair of Chinese servants bring Orpheus champagne while
he is instructed not to try and understand everything. Back
downstairs, Mrs Death orders Cegeste to 'get up'. And, in a
moment that is more James Brown than Lazarus, I would say,
he rises from the dead. He is now the servant of her who is
Death. Magically the others go through a mirror which, despite
his efforts, Orpheus cannot penetrate. Instead, he falls asleep
and awakes to find himself lying outside on a sandy dune.
However, continuity with the House of Death is maintained by
the presence of the Rolls-Royce and its chauffeur – Heurtebise.
Orpheus gets into the car. Clearly, he has to return to the
'upper' world to consolidate his experience and what he has
learned so far.

From the House of Death, Orpheus is returned to the 'real'
world. But as this occurs after his falling asleep, the movement between the two worlds of 'reality' and 'elsewhere'
– or, conscious and unconscious life – is made ambiguous.
The 'real world', like the prosaic, 'mature' rationality, gets
toppled from its place on top of a hierarchy, which conven-
tionally places less importance on unconscious life – another
lesson the precociously grown-up have to learn. As Jung
noted, this is as true for a culture that assumes a maturity
it has not yet earned through experience as it is for the
individual. What is not known to consciousness, such as
the inner journey and the otherness of death – which in life
gets carried by the otherness of the unconscious – sit side by
side with outer achievement and living a life. Just as the
bikers, the bringers of death, ride side by side with the Rolls-
Royce car throughout the whole narrative of the film.

In our times, Jung emphasised how we underestimate or ignore the unconscious at our peril. He spoke of how the over-valuing of conscious rationality produces a compensatory reaction from the unconscious that can be poetic and creative or impulsive and destructive. Jung's influence has probably been greatest since 1945 and at the time of the movie's first release he was writing about the threat of the atomic bomb, analogising this to an explosive unconscious. Elsewhere in post-war culture, the poets were fulfilling their Orphic duty – compensating for a one-sided, over-rational consciousness – that had led a previous generation to war, dominance, prejudice and exploitation, with the energy of Dionysian response.

Back in 'reality' as Orpheus is being driven home, we cut to Eurydice, his wife, who has been ringing round the hotels to find the woman in the Rolls who went off with her husband. A journalist turns up to speak to Orpheus, and Eurydice lies to him saying Orpheus is lying asleep upstairs. The lie gets exposed when Orpheus turns up in the Rolls and brushes off the journalist.

This moment plays on words and meanings which refer to 'lying down', telling untruths, and the lyre – itself associated in myth with trickery and lying words[10] – as an instrument to accompany poetry. This connects with what I have just said about the sort of attention we pay to the unconscious in our contemporary lives. I have recently talked this over with a client who was questioning the idea of 'lying on the couch'. Her concern was that by lying down – ostensibly to help the release of unconscious material as many psychoanalysts would recommend – she would be facilitating 'lying' to me, meaning she might be avoidant and more resistant than when we were sitting face to face. Again this strikes me as a reversal of the hierarchy between conscious and unconscious that depth psychology introduced at the turn of the last century, but in the form in which Jung recommended. He rejected the assumption that lying supine could guarantee better release of unconscious material, and made the case for a more human situation of talking face to face. Sitting face to face need not in itself cause us to slip into an unhelpful, non-therapeutic relationship or dialogue of a purely social – or even, intellectualising – type. With the right attention, a fully therapeutic and psychological attitude can still be maintained in such circumstances and offers equal possibility for awareness of unconscious material. Far from ensuring *authentic* unconscious material, lying down (aggrandised in the trade as: 'using the couch') may offer just as many opportunities for avoidance and resistance. This consideration may help us with what happens next in Cocteau's film – and especially the way he films it.

> *Eurydice is delighted to see Orpheus but he is angry that Eurydice has brought a police superintendent and 'a girl I dislike' – Aglaonice – into his house. At first we see the detective and the girl from Orpheus' point of view but higher, as if he is far taller than them. Eurydice comes into the shot to complete the trio, but, strangely, she rises up from the very bottom of the screen, and appears in close-up while the other two remain at a distance in medium-shot. It is as if she is rising from the bottom of Orpheus' unconscious and serves as a premonition of her later rising back to life when Orpheus retrieves her from Death.*
>
> *Eurydice says she has 'good news' but Orpheus does not wait to hear it, preoccupied as he is with his experiences and, now, the mysterious poetry coming through the car radio. He goes up to sleep. He steps on a baby's bootie as he leaves the room and – in the best movie tradition of 'show don't tell' – we realise Eurydice's 'news'. We see that Orpheus' devotion to his new muse in the radio means he has a 'replacement' for Eurydice because we now see him climbing down a ladder from the upstairs bedroom to go to the car and its radio in the garage.*
>
> *Meanwhile, back in the kitchen, the chauffeur comes in to see Eurydice. He says he is really a penniless student called Heurtebise. Over soft flute music, Eurydice asks him about*

Orpheus' missing night and she confesses her fears: 'He's handsome and famous. It's a miracle if he stays faithful.'

Whether we see the so-called sexual revolution of the 1960s as a blessing or a curse, it is undeniably one of the most significant social changes of the last 60 years. The technology of the birth pill freed women from risk of pregnancy in a method that was under their own control for once. But an increase in sexual freedom for heterosexual men[11] and women made little difference when it came to a greater tolerance for male promiscuity over female promiscuity or 'sexual freedom' which remained less valued in women, as it had for centuries before the pill. As a woman, you still had to worry more about your man going off. As with Orpheus, the lyrical heroes of the new Dionysian age of the 60s and 70s were cock-thrusting young men,[12] made even more attractive through a new feminised stance that allowed them to be beautiful and rejecting of conventional masculinity, while no one could doubt their heterosexual intent and appeal. Only the straights thought they were 'queer' or 'homos' – the young girls knew exactly which side their bread was buttered on, thank you. This was another way to register change and protest against the old regime. When it comes to the *senex* values of the old order that the *puer* wishes to address, there are none more sensitive than gender identity and the 'certainty' of sexual orientation with their assumption of the immutable, 'natural' and 'biological' now revealed as a veneer over a vulnerable, culture-based fluidity.

The chauffeur hates the smell of gas because, he blurts, 'That's how I committed suicide.' Quickly he corrects himself with 'How I attempted suicide'. Following this we see how Mrs Death has returned to watch Orpheus, stalking him in his sleep. Next day, Orpheus, Eurydice and Heurtebise are listening to radio messages in the car. Orpheus writes down the words, 'The bird sings with its fingers . . . once . . . I repeat'. He wants inspiration for his poetry, he needs a muse – but Eurydice wants him to pay attention to her pregnancy and their future child. It looks like the old creative-work versus home-and-wife split! Orpheus has to go to town and as Heurtebise gets Orpheus' sports two-seater – because Orpheus is 'too nervous to drive' – the bikers of Death zoom past on the road.

There is something about the bikers with their retrograde aggressive masculinity which, during the 1940s and 50s and later in the form of California's Hell's Angels, constituted the aggressive male shadow for the peace 'n' love 60s. Their image was enough of a threat in itself – while Americans could enjoy Marlon Brando in *The Wild Ones* from 1953, Britain only lifted the ban on the film in 1968. It would have been far better to integrate rather than censor what the bikers represent.[13] Coming in the form of a backlash, it suggests that any new realm inspired by the Dionysian needs to be more substantial if it is to maintain itself successfully. Such a new realm needs to rediscover the more positive *senex* values that had made the previous era robust in its time. In a rock concert at the Altamont Speedway, Hell's Angels acting as 'security' in a parody of 'what it means to be a man', murdered a fan close to the stage where The Rolling Stones were playing 'Sympathy for the Devil' – an event that stands starkly in the shadow of the peaceful success of Woodstock in the previous year. The 60s needed to grow up fast. Death is real, Orpheus, or, as the old slogan said of life: 'This is not a rehearsal'.

In the empty town Orpheus chases the woman representing Death through streets and passages. The few people see him but cannot help. The majority are all young, especially the fans who stall him for autographs, predicting how they would with the Beatles in A Hard Day's Night *(1964, dir. Dick Lester), not due on cinema screens for another 14 years.*

A newspaper has published an article with the poetry that Orpheus has gleaned from the radio. Scandal ensues when it is revealed that these are not Orpheus' words and images but Cegeste's poems! All are shocked to think that Orpheus would plagiarise the poems of the vanished – presumed dead – young man. Orpheus is after all 'a national figure', we are told.

Back home, as Orpheus takes down more poetry from the radio, Eurydice sets out on a bicycle to see her friend and gets knocked off by the bikers in their second hit-and-run. The chauffeur Heurtebise brings her body upstairs to lie on the bed where Death and Cegeste illicitly visit her from the Underworld.

We see Cegeste broadcasting his inspiring words at the portable radio transmitter: 'The widows weeds refresh the sun' – more poetry for Orpheus to pick up 'on the air' of the car radio. Here is Cocteau underlining how it has been the technology of electronic communications that has driven the rise of Orphic popular forms, from the radio in his day to stereophonic sound, powerful amplification and digital recording in our own time.[14]

Death gets upset when Heurtebise suggests that she is in love with Orpheus. Heurtebise tries to get Orpheus away from his compulsive listening to the radio – his sad addiction to his new 'muse'. Heurtebise talks seriously, emphasising the danger Eurydice is in, but Orpheus says it is merely a ruse, once again she is 'lying', she is putting on an act, he says, and he will not come upstairs to see her. And upon Orpheus' rejection of empathic concern for his wife, Mrs Death and Cegeste take Eurydice (as spirit) through the mirror into the realm of Death.

Orpheus is shown Eurydice lying dead on the bed and cries the crucial lines, 'This nightmare just won't end! Wake me up!', followed by, 'I thought I knew about death but I didn't.'

At last comes the moment when Orpheus confronts what is important about his life. He has for too long dedicated himself to being the poet, the lyrical voice that speaks to the fans, but ignores his wife and the new life growing inside her. He has to make the journey to retrieve her from Death. His are the last of the 'strongly middle-aged values' the University of Wisconsin uncovered in 1950. It is the generation of Cegeste that will take the Dionysian lyric form forward. Orpheus – like the Beat Poets, Ginsberg, Ferlinghetti and Kerouac in the late 40s – has laid the groundwork but he will be sacrificed for his efforts.

With Heurtebise commanding 'Don't try to understand just believe', and leading the way, Orpheus at last goes through the mirror. On the Other Side the dead walk about not knowing their state – one sells window-panes with a mournful cry.

Mrs Death is in trouble with the judges of Hades, however, and charged with bringing back Cegeste and Eurydice. Orpheus arrives with a gay leap through the mirror. When it comes to Orpheus' appearance as a witness he is asked whether he is a poet or writer. Someone jokes, 'he writes without being a writer' – thus condensing the revolution in language to a phrase. Death admits to loving Orpheus and going to his room – she asks Orpheus for a pen to sign her confession. 'Oh I forgot you're not a writer', she quips. In a further extension of the myth, Eurydice comes before the judges with Heurtebise who confesses he loves her and signs his own confession. Orpheus and Death embrace with words of love, then the judges of Hades give their decision.

Death and Heurtebise are freed on probation. Orpheus is freed on the condition he tells nothing of what he has seen and, in the famous clincher, 'Eurydice is freed on the condition Orpheus never again looks upon her. One look and she is lost forever!' comes the command.

Heurtebise leads Orpheus and Eurydice out of the Underworld to ensure the conditions are fulfilled. Orpheus keeps his eyes tight shut. Back at their own house, Orpheus picks up a letter, which accuses him of being a thief and a murderer. The Maenads, in Cocteau's story played by the young café crowd, are now close and want their sacrifice. Orpheus and Eurydice are back home comically trying to avoid Orpheus looking at her ('Hide under the table!' 'Look out he's coming!' exclaims Heurtebise.) They try to adjust to their conditions of survival – they even attempt a marital tiff, arguing back to back, but as soon as Orpheus gets passionate he tries to turn to her and Heurtebise has to grab his head to stop him. Eurydice wakes him in bed but luckily the lights black out before he opens his eyes to see her. But finally, Eurydice gets in the car where Orpheus is once again listening to the radio. She gets his *attention, he looks up and, as he glimpses her in the rear-view mirror, she vanishes.*

But now the Maenads have arrived. A protest starts up outside the house – the crowd of young men and women are reacting to Orpheus' alleged plagiarising of their new hero's work. There is shouting and the insistent sound of loud jazz drumming.

Cocteau's scene predicts the Bishop of Woolwich writing in *The Times* of London in 1955 who, after riots in the cinema, advocated a ban on the film *Blackboard Jungle* with the words, 'The hypnotic rhythm and the wild gestures have a maddening effect on a rhythm-loving age group and the result of its impact is the relaxing of all self-control'.[15] In the case of Cocteau's Orpheus such a lack of self-control leads to his destruction by the crowd. Now, at last, he can join Eurydice and retire from his role as poet. But this is only to make way for an initiation and celebration of the new wave begun by his successor, the new young lyricist Cegeste. In the Greek myth, it is the decapitated head of Orpheus landing on the shores of Lesbos that initiates the start of lyric poetry. In our time, as Marek Kohn observes,[16] the Bishop of Woolwich seems to have unwittingly 'grasped the dynamics of popular music for the next half century'.

Orpheus gets shot with Heurtebise's discarded gun and the police arrive to arrest the rioting young people just as they did at the start of the film. For the last time, the black leather bikers return and drag Orpheus' body into the Rolls and ride side-saddle as Heurtebise drives off. This time, as he heads for Death's mansion, it is Orpheus, not Cegeste, who is lying dead on the back seat of the car. And although there is a sentimental reuniting of Orpheus and Eurydice to come, the film is over. We have got the message. We remember the beginning when we see the end. Just as Orpheus remembers his first visit to Death when he returns on this occasion – not as a guest this time, but as the real thing.

And Cocteau's film is all about the importance of remembering. Reversing the unremembered, dismembered soul. It is all about putting ourselves back together. Just as our psychological and cultural reflections seek to put the story of our times back together. Orpheus remembers he is mortal – despite the immortality of poetry and gods. He remembers he has a human love for a woman Eurydice – which he needs to recall. He remembers he is in the world of ordinary human desires – the crowd that cause his death – not solely in the world of his muse – the radio, which he could not resist, and which led to both his and Eurydice's death. In one of the original versions of the Orpheus myth he is dismembered by a crowd of Maenads. They constitute a specifically female ferocious retaliation that Cocteau fails to offer; Eurydice is mild in her complaints. The crowd of young people that kill him in the film *Orphee* are both genders: in our times the protest that requires sacrifice, the dis-membering, the final dis-assembly by bullet of Orpheus' life, is energised through a generational division, not one based on gender.

In all our activities, death precedes rebirth. Popular culture was reborn for a new generation in the early 50s. Maybe it was 5 July, 1954 when Elvis recorded 'That's All Right (Mama)'; maybe it was when Wham-O produced the first frisbee in the USA on 13 January, 1957. Certainly it was all in place by the time William Burroughs published *Naked Lunch* in 1959. In 1961 Dylan played his first pro gig at Gerde's Folk City, New York and John F. Kennedy, in his inaugural address, uttered the awkward yet beautiful lyric, 'Ask not what your country can do for you – ask what you can do for your country'. Thirty-four months later, he too would be dead. But the age continued. What began in the 50s and became known as the 60s – this Orphic age without Orpheus – continued.

It continues.

Notes

1 BBC (2001) Radio 4, *Back Row*, 'Psychoanalysis and film', broadcast 3 November, produced by S. Hughes.

2 Ibid.
3 As in the case of D-Day remembered once again on its sixtieth anniversary on 6 June 2004, 'lest we forget'.
4 Humphries, P. (2004) 'All shook up', *BBC History Magazine*, 5(7),
   pp. 14–18.
5 Note: from now on I will use the convention of putting in italics the
   events of the film, to distinguish them from my comments in roman.
6 1998, dir. Gary Ross.
7 The 'Sixties' seem to begin in 1957 with the publication of Jack
   Kerouac's *On the Road*, and end in the early 70s with the end of the
   Vietnam War.
8 Salinger, J.D. (1951) *The Catcher in the Rye*. Harmondsworth: Penguin.
9 We could be hearing 'The ghost of electricity howls in the bones of
   her face' (Bob Dylan, 1965, 'Visions of Johanna', *Blonde on Blonde*, CBS
   records).
10 As in the myth of Hermes, a trickster, who stole Apollo's cattle only
   to soothe him into forgiveness by playing him a tune on the lyre. The
   lyre is also strikingly similar to the modern guitar that has been so
   central to the rise of the lyric and the poetic since 1954 when Elvis cut
   his first single in Sun Studios, Memphis. Perhaps we need to consider
   the degree to which popular lyrical culture has been merely soothing
   and hence 'lying' and the degree to which it has offered a radical
   challenge to dominant consciousness as the rest of this section suggests.
11 Gay men got their sexuality and were legalised in this period too of
   course, which has been a parallel freedom with parallel mixed results.
12 I am thinking, of course, of Elvis, Mick Jagger, Jim Morrison, Jimi
   Hendrix and, especially, Robert Plant of Led Zepplin. The beginning
   of the end started with David Bowie's sexual ambiguity and characterisation of the rock star as pastiche in his Ziggy Stardust, leading
   to pastiches of Jagger in Steve Tyler (Aerosmith) and others, and the
   rock singer as gay man in Queen's Freddy Mercury – note the name,
   a trickster reversal of the 'feminine-yet-aggressively-heterosexual-
   groupie-banger' of the launch years of rock.
13 Just as sexuality in literature had been accepted in 1960 with the failure
   of the charge of obscenity against Penguin Books for publishing *Lady
   Chatterley's Lover* by D.H. Lawrence.
14 When Orpheus and the chauffeur journey to the Underworld to
   retrieve Eurydice later, there are characters wandering in the limbo of
   Hades. One of these carries window-panes on his back and is calling
   out 'Windows! Windows!' – it gives me a chill to even point this out!
   Did Cocteau dream the future?
15 Humphries, op. cit., p. 16.
16 Kohn, M. quoted by Humphries, ibid.

21 grams[1]

Life as a human being is a life that ends in death. We are not exempt. Our being ceases to be and, depending on your world view and religious belief, what is left of the being 'goes' somewhere else.

Just about every human culture and, I bet, every human being, has a theory of what post-life is. For thousands of years, many humans believed that post-life was a chance to get into another being and try life all over again. The trouble is it is a bit like the Christian heaven and hell deal. Only if you did good stuff – moral, sincere acts with integrity – would you get a chance to return as a human. Actually, as a male human. Actually, as a male human with a degree of opportunity, robust health, a safe environment, solvent parents and all you would wish for your own great-grandchildren. Except the male bit. That is there because there is a hierarchy in this post-life view which says the best lived life gives the top rebirth through the accumulation of karma produced by good acts, and the range of rebirths available starts with 'male human', closely followed by 'female human', and all the way down through dog, elephant, halibut, plankton to gnat. This rebirth theory is careful to emphasise that it is not *you* as the historical ego you and yours were familiar with that carries on 'in the body of' another creature. It is more the case that the acts and life you lived inevitably get attracted into a suitable form for 'your' rebirth. Though exactly what qualifications are required to get the plankton rebirth it is hard to say. As for the evidence, presumably the way youngsters can be found 'remembering' stuff from a previous life as a human is far easier to understand and accept than if they were trying to describe their previous incarnation as a newt. But how the myriad of non-human creatures achieve sufficient moral acts to get themselves up the reincarnation scale is also quite beyond me.

The fact is we cannot conceive of our own death. Let alone what happens after. There seems to be ample evidence of so-called 'near death' experiences and these appear to have a good deal in common across a range of people which suggests they are a typically human or archetypal experience. No one, not even a ghost as far as I have heard, has come back to let us know what post-life is like. From what ghosts do 'say' it seems they are stuck in a dream version of the life they once lived as if they have no idea they are dead. If our present-day denial or aversion to death continues, I predict many more humans will get stuck in this post-life limbo they make for themselves. Animals, it is reckoned, while they know pain just as we do, do not know death as an existential fact. Or rather, as the non-existential fact it really is.

Some Buddhist theory puts it quite succinctly. We are like a bundle of sticks bound good and tight together while alive. Mind, body and soul in all its varied parts keep together through the aliveness of the organism that is us. In fact the bound togetherness is the aliveness itself. With death, the binding breaks. The sticks fall apart and there is no longer a living organism. Just a pile of sticks. The sticks are not 'me'. It was the whole sticks-bound-together Gestalt moving around in the world that was 'me'. That is why we talk about the *corpse*. The body that spoke and acted and was thus a human being is the same entity as what, post-life, we now call the corpse. For quite a while after death it is the same organism. But it is not a *being*, it is a corpse. What has happened? For the Buddhists, the sticks are unbound and have fallen apart. Same sticks – they are just not bound into a being any more. Other humans and cultures like to see this change as if something has *left the body*. We use the words 'departed' and 'she is gone' and he has 'moved on' as if the body was a house and the human that lived there has gone to find another 'home'. The Buddhist idea says all that has 'gone' is the binding of the sticks. Not the binding itself, that is still there like the sticks are. But the binding as a verb, as in the *held-togetherness* of the whole bound-together-sticks phenomenon. That is what's gone. Apparently it weighs 21 grams.

Note

1 *21 Grams*, directed by Alejandro Gonzalez-Inarritu was released in 2003. The tagline on the poster reads, 'How much does life weigh?'

11

Surviving: a child being human

Human life ends in death. This book on human being started with the way we define ourselves by comparison with animals and now I am talking about us a bunch of sticks. In these times, we think we have made so much of human life – and feel so entitled to celebrate our success and progress – that human death has seldom been so hard to accept and include in our vision of ourselves. We are still baffled as if it was the most unlikely thing on the planet. We do not seem to know what is more ridiculous: the fact that all these lives end in death, or the fact that we have such a hard job believing it. We are always so surprised. Or we think it so 'unfair', as if we should be exempt from this aspect of being. One of the most powerful qualities of our human being – and of anything that lives – is the desire to survive, to continue being.

This desire to 'cheat death' as though we were in some sort of card game (or chess, of course) where we can win through our cleverness, is the stuff of so many heroic tales. The factual ones do indeed show extraordinary human courage and spirit, like the young man who got his arm caught in the cleft of two boulders and, after three days, decided there was nothing for it but to hack his arm off or die of thirst and starvation. He did hack his arm off and – astonishingly – walked to safety and survived.[1] Just as the mountaineer lost down a glacier and left for dead also survived and became the subject of the marvellous movie,

Touching the Void.[2] Both of them not only lived, they also lived to tell their tale and to publish it as a book and a film.

Equally courageous but less publicised are those who survive serious violence or illness and also manage to continue their lives. Some, like those attacked in war or on the street, may remain traumatised long after the wounds to the body have healed. Once medicine and surgery have done their work, these people need further human help to heal the *soul* – without which their being may be permanently scarred.[3] Survivors of train crashes and crowd disasters have also benefited from talking through their trauma.

For the psychotherapist, work with such traumatised people inevitably involves matters of life and death, and survival. Although what I am about to describe is not typical of all work with trauma, I am finishing this book with an example of psychotherapy with a young boy that did involve a matter of life and death. When psychotherapists help people like this they usually know what they are going to be working with in advance, but this time I was taken by surprise. I once worked as a counsellor at a primary school where I was referred children who were disruptive in class and the playground, who did not settle to their work or in relationships with others, and who clearly had a degree of emotional conflict, which was influencing their behaviour. These children were usually of average ability or above, and they were usually boys. The girls tended to show their unhappiness through withdrawal while the boys 'acted out' as the phrase goes. Such acting-out was disruptive not only to the boys but to the school as a whole, so they tended to be prioritised for counselling attention. (Since I finished this work, the girls' different ways of expressing their needs have been recognised and given equal attention and help.)

One such boy, who I will call Keith, was referred to me with a typical profile. He would wander about the classroom and not settle to tasks given by the teacher; he would break pencils to call attention to his need for a new one; and he would spoil other children's work when required to work cooperatively. Keith was 10 years old when we first met; he came from a working-class background and lived with his mother and a younger sister. He was a little smaller than other boys of his age, with dark curly hair and a serious expression. He had a wiry physique and loved to play football on the green outside the flats where he lived. His father lived elsewhere and Keith only saw him from time to time. Keith's mother was white, his mother's boyfriend was a young black man, and Keith himself seemed about one quarter mixed race. He did not particularly identify himself as black, although he indicated his father was mixed race. I met Keith's little sister (aged 5 and from a different father), his mother and sometimes her boyfriend on occasional home visits but I did not meet his father. During the time I was seeing Keith, his mother became pregnant by her current boyfriend, Craig.

I had been introduced to Keith at the end of the summer term and we began our sessions properly in the following September. I had discussed with him why he thought the headteacher had recommended we meet for sessions and I showed him the room and the materials he might use. I have found children prefer to be doing something rather than just talking. While talking takes less of a priority than it does with adults, children are keen to draw, write stories, play with puppets and models using a sand-tray or the dolls' house or the garage, and to make objects from modelling clay and cardboard. While they are 'playing' like this, they feel more free to bring up what is on their mind or use the picture or model to help get across their thoughts and feelings. They also reveal a good deal of their inner world in the pictures and the models they make.

Once we returned to the school in September, however, the work with Keith took on a very different quality. At the end of the summer, Keith had been diagnosed with Hodgkin's lymphoma, a type of cancer, which started with a lump on his neck. I was told – and I trust he was told too – that there was a 90 per cent survival rate if this cancer is treated early, but it was still a life-threatening disease which required regular chemotherapy treatment for many weeks. At our first

Figure 11.1 Tree, House, Person and Colourful Tree

session I asked Keith how he was feeling with this news. He kept his responses quite practical, as he would throughout our sessions: everyone on his council estate (public housing project) had been told of his condition by his mother, he said, and his biggest regret was that he was no longer allowed outside to play football – which he loved. His chemotherapy treatment required there to be a thin tube (a Pick line) permanently inserted into a major artery adjacent to his heart and physical sports risked disturbing this line in a dangerous way.

We went on to do the drawing exercise I ask all children to complete on a first meeting (and again after every ten weeks or so to see what may change in the picture). I ask them to draw a tree, a house and a person, however they like. Keith drew the picture you see in Figure 11.1. There is a house drawn in black and white, and there is a tree drawn very colourfully. 'Where is the person?' I asked Keith. He pointed out the person was at the window of the house looking out. 'Trapped inside like he'd been told off by his mum', Keith said. Without saying anything, I guessed that the colourful tree and the monochrome house reflected different aspects of Keith – an optimistic, growing side and a depressed,

203

forlorn one. I asked Keith to tell me about the tree and he said it had strong roots. He said, 'It's a good tree for a tree house', and added, 'I could have done a shrivelled brown tree'. Then, feeling inspired, he drew the very large colourful tree on the right side of Figure 11.1 which filled up a whole piece of paper. This felt like a good sign that Keith had a strong spirit – depicted in the rich, green foliage and the strong, brown tree-trunk drawing up life from the earth – which would help him survive the cancer. He drew a platform behind the branches to show the 'tree house' within, but afterwards he looked at his picture and said, 'It looks like a monster . . . screaming'.

I next saw Keith a week later. He told me that he had had a dream of winning a thousand pounds 'against the odds' on a game called 'Cluedo Lotto'. I recognised in this a communication about the odds on his surviving the cancer and the guesswork involved. I gently pursued this idea but Keith was reluctant to say more. It seems it was enough that I showed I understood his anxiety. Then Keith asked if he could make a model with the modelling clay. This material was to become his primary form of communicating his inner world from now on. He made a model of a Ninja warrior, which you can see in Figure 11.2. I asked him about the Ninja and he associated it to a story he had seen or heard about a Ninja warrior who was a grandfather and who had heroically saved some children. We found a large, tin biscuit-box for the finished model and put his name on it. Keith placed the Ninja warrior carefully inside and we put the box at the back of a filing cabinet for safe-keeping.

When I saw Keith the next week he was wearing a woollen hat although it was a mild day and we were indoors. Keith's mother, having heard that the chemotherapy would cause his hair to fall out gradually, had decided to have all his hair shaved off.[4] Keith did not comment particularly on this, but it struck me that the permanent woollen hat now made him conspicuously known for his cancer just as his absence from outdoor play and the informing of all the neighbours had done. He went on to make a second model. He started by

Figure 11.2 Ninja Warrior

Figure 11.3 Craig

making 'Just a normal man', he said, but then he changed his mind and made a head-and-shoulders model (Figure 11.3) of 'Craig' – his mother's boyfriend – looking very angry with staring eyes and a protruding tongue. While he was modelling this, I played with the clay too and found I had made

205

Figure 11.4 Desolate Tree

a coiled-up snake.[5] At the end of the session Keith put all the models in his box where they made a scene of the snake scaring Craig being fought off by the Ninja. It was not clear whether the Ninja was fighting off the snake or fighting off Craig.

I did not see Keith until three weeks had passed, during which time he had stayed in hospital for his chemotherapy. He spoke about his six-day stay and the antibiotics he had been given and the sickness and vomiting he had had to bear. He drew a new picture of a house, a tree and a person. You can see this in Figure 11.4. This was a far bleaker picture than the one drawn at the beginning of term. Keith agreed that it showed 'sad things', but for myself I was worried that the tree that had once been so strong and colourful was now monochrome like the rest of the picture; now it had no leaves and looked like it was dying. I was reminded of photographs of a ravaged battle-front in World War I. However, the person was now out of the house and standing with arms stretched with a suggestion of, 'I am here! This is me'. Perhaps the spirit was still alive.

Figure 11.5 The Two Snakes

In the same session, Keith looked at the models we had in the box and made another snake to go with mine (a far superior model as you can see!). His snake was a cobra complete with hood and deadly fangs all carefully crafted. The two snakes are photographed together in Figure 11.5. Put together in this way, they reminded me of Asklepios and the origins of healing and medicine which remain with us today in the *caduceus* – the medical doctors' symbol of two snakes entwined around the staff of Asklepios, the god of healing.[6]

In the same session Keith went on to make what he called, at first, 'a baby shark'. He got into this image and carried on until he had made the model you see in Figure 11.6. If you could see the original colour photograph you would see how Keith's baby shark became this large, bright blue, ferocious creature with a human body in its jaws and red blood dripping down.

The next week Keith made the model of an old lady with a walking stick you see in Figure 11.7. 'It is my sister', Keith said. This was puzzling because his sister was only 5, but I think I knew what he meant: he was wondering if he would

Figure 11.6 Ferocious Shark

Figure 11.7 The Old Lady

live long enough to see her as an old woman. 'It's her as a grumpy old lady', he told me, 'I wonder what she'll be like when she's old . . .'

I had been playing with the clay and had made a man's head. Keith took over the model and made what you can

Figure 11.8 Rasta Father

see in Figure 11.8. He added the dreadlocks, the arms and the guitar after talking about how his dad had 'sort of Rasta hair' and that he played the guitar. Again I sensed Keith's awareness of the generations and the risk to his own survival to produce the next generation. He said, 'It's a very sick Rasta man; he's going to throw up at any minute'. He had talked earlier of the vomiting which was a side-effect of his chemotherapy but then he said, 'Look – he's like Jesus'. Keith seemed intuitively aware of how his inner resources were needed to complement all the efforts of the doctors. His image and his comments expressed his need for parental strength and protection, his need for someone to heal him, and his awareness of sickness in the sense of both the vomiting and the actual cancer.

The following week Keith talked again about his chemo-therapy, how long it was taking and how many more weeks and the number of treatments he had left to go. He was 'counting the days'. On the surface, this was Keith hating all the side-effects of the chemotherapy, from the vomiting through to the loss of playing football. He was dying for it all to be over. But what he did not speak about was a parallel 'counting the days until it's all over'. He never directly expressed a fear he would die (really 'dying for it all to end'), or even fear about death itself, but this fear does appear in many of the images and concerns he brought. Ernest Becker, in *The Denial of Death*,[7] points out how psychoanalytic ideas about what disturbs us have moved on from Freud's early ideas of repression and, instead of being overwhelmed by instinctual urges, humans – especially children – are regarded as suffering a more general existential anxiety about the security of their being in the world:

> We have achieved a remarkably faithful understanding of what really bothers the child, how life is really too much for him, how he has to avoid too much thought, too much perception, too much *life*. And at the same time, how he has to avoid the death that rumbles behind and underneath every carefree activity, that looks over his shoulder as he plays.[8]

Keith made an evocative model of a tramp and his dog that you can see in Figure 11.9. Keith's mother seldom took him anywhere far from his neighbourhood. Journeying up to the city would have brought him many new experiences like seeing people sleeping rough on the streets. Keith told me he thought the tramp was lonely, which is how Keith said he himself felt when he was in his hospital room. I noticed how the tramp has been given a dog to keep him company. The tramp is keeping himself warm with a blanket, and the dog has been given a blanket too. The tramp seems to be doing his best to look after himself, and to look after his dog who is as important for his well-being as the warm blanket is for his body. The third item in the model is a tiny begging cup Keith made for the tramp. Despite being destitute and lonely, the tramp is doing what he can to see himself through.[9]

In the same session, Keith made another model, shown in Figure 11.10. He said it was 'a woman being sick'. Later he said it was his mother. For Keith, one of the most uncom-

Figure 11.9 Tramp and Dog

Figure 11.10 Woman Being Sick

fortable and distressing effects of his chemotherapy was the vomiting it induced. When he made this model I thought it was a way of getting his mother to share some of his distress and discomfort by having her do the vomiting too. I only found out later that she was pregnant and having morning sickness herself. It may be that Keith was also expressing how he felt his mother had an insufficient capacity to share the burden of his suffering. She herself was only 26 and, coming on top of her pregnancy, Keith's illness and the hospital visits that it required was yet 'one more thing she had to worry about'.

Another three weeks passed until I saw Keith again. He was now over halfway through his chemotherapy sessions and it was two weeks until Christmas. Keith seemed more optimistic this time. He spoke about football and different team formations. He said he had had a dream about meeting a famous football player he admired. I suggested he wrote to the player at his club but Keith said he was too shy. The next week when I saw him, I brought in some writing paper with the image of a footballer on it and he took it home and wrote the letter. We posted it from the office at school.

After the Christmas holiday, Keith returned announcing there was only one more chemotherapy session to go. It seems his cancer was responding to the treatment. During this time the movie *Alive*[10] was shown on TV. It is a true story of the rugby football team whose aeroplane crashed high up in the Andes in South America. It seems the plane split in half and many passengers died immediately, some were badly hurt and died later, but several more survived uninjured. Keith made a model of the plane as it crashes into the mountain, which you can see in Figure 11.11. The colours are white with streaks of red signifying blood and death rather like in his model of the shark (Figure 11.6).

As the survivors waited for help to come, they used part of the plane's fuselage for shelter and scavenged for what food and fuel they could retrieve from the crash. They buried the dead in the snow. After some time the food ran out and the survivors faced starvation or the unthinkable alternative – to eat the flesh of their dead fellow human beings. They decided that, if they wished to live, they had little alternative and survived their ordeal in this way until the snows melted and two of them travelled down the mountain to get help for the rest of the survivors.

Figure 11.11 Plane Crash

Keith made a second model inspired by this story. In Figure 11.12 we are looking down on the scene in the plane fuselage, which now contains the survivors, huddled together under blankets for warmth, protection and survival (the real fuselage was intact and only open at one end, but Keith removed the top section so that we could see them all inside). Both these models express and hold much of the horror of Keith's journey and his fight against cancer. They also carry many of the elements we have seen in the earlier models. The two models of the plane, one destructive and the other protective, remind me of the two snakes (Figure 11.5): one is benign and one is aggressive. They are paired opposites like the poison and the antidote, or the disease and the remedy. Even though I made one of these snakes myself, it was Keith who made the image a *pair* by modelling the second snake and putting them together. Together they form the *pair-for-healing* in which Keith was always a participant.[11]

The danger, blood and horror of the shark attack (Figure 11.6) is present as the plane crashes into the mountain, splitting apart and flinging its passengers out to their deaths.

213

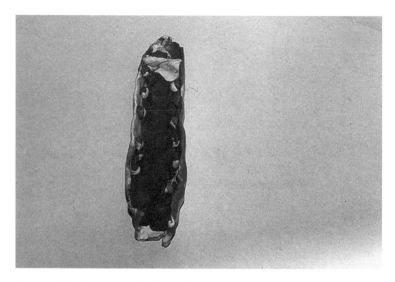

Figure 11.12 Survivors Shelter in the Fuselage

The protection afforded the tramp, the company of another living creature and his blanket (Figure 11.9) reappear in the model of the survivors huddled together in the fuselage. Close to death, they keep each other warm in the corpse of the plane. Through these images Keith conveyed to me – and to himself – how he was surviving his own ordeal. The survivors turned the deaths of their fellow humans into a means of staying alive. Keith turned the threat of his own death into images that, on one hand, conveyed the horror and fear of dying and, on the other, expressed the spirit and security of surviving.

No one can really imagine their own death. How can we imagine an experience that, when the actual *moment of death* comes, is, by definition, not one of *life's* experiences? We are asking ourselves to imagine *the end of life's experiences*. The end of all experiences. The end of being a human being. Getting very close to death, anticipating the real end of life like Keith and many in his position do – letting it sink in for what it really is – and then to carry on living: this delivers a greater experience. Perhaps we all need a version of such an experience to live as fully alive human beings. As Becker says, 'Life can suck one up, sap his energies, submerge him, take away his self-control . . . load him up with new responsibilities which need great strength to bear', but there is more to life than 'life', 'Above all', Becker continues, 'there is the danger of a slip-up, an accident, a chance disease, and of course of death, the final sucking up, the total submergence and negation'.[12]

Once, I was at the end of my garden, sitting among the tangle of brambles and overgrown grass and bushes and the thought occurred to me: 'Nature doesn't care about us at all'. The natural world goes on doing its thing, pursuing its own being; grass grows as grass, brambles keep on growing as brambles. Since time immemorial, we humans have both used and exploited and conserved and cultivated the natural environment. We always have some sort of definite attitude or relationship to it. But nature does not care about us. Cancers do not care about us. Earthquakes do not care about us. Human beings care. *We* care about us. Caring about ourselves and caring about the world – however that works out – is what we do. That is our human being.

And Keith? Keith survived.

Notes

1 I am referring to the story of Alan Ralston, recently published in *Between the Rock and a Hard Place* (Simon & Schuster, 2004).

2 *Touching the Void* (2003, dir Kevin Macdonald).

3 Working through mental conflict and distress by talking with another human being is the treatment offered by many of the psychotherapies. This type of help has its roots in the treatment of soldiers traumatised by warfare. It was W.H.R. Rivers who brought this type of treatment to the attention of the British and American medical establishment during the World War I by pioneering a type of psychoanalytic 'talking cure' with military officers suffering from what was then called 'shell-shock'. Among his patients at the Craiglockhart Hospital in Edinburgh were Siegfried Sassoon and Wilfred Owen, two well-known literary figures, which, among other things, raised the profile of this method.

The story of these men and the regime at Craiglockhart has been enshrined in a fictional version as a film, *Regeneration* (1997, dir. G. MacKinnon). Called *Behind The Lines* in the USA and *Renaissance* in Canada, it is based on the book *Regeneration* by Pat Barker (Penguin, 1992). See also: Fussell, P. (1975) *The Great War and Modern Memory*. Oxford: Oxford University Press.

4 I am reminded of Stewart Brand's comment in *The Clock of the Long Now: Time and Responsibility* (Weidenfeld & Nicolson, 1999) that bad things happen quickly and good things happen over time. The sudden shaving of Keith's head was a further 'bad' marker of his cancer diagnosis, while the gradual hair loss that accompanied chemotherapy was a marker of, hopefully, his gradual healing.

5 The famous psychoanalyst and paediatrician D.W. Winnicott was one of the first to develop a method of working with children where the therapist and child would both contribute to making an image in a way that resembles the exchange of conversation in talking therapies with adults. This method involves the therapist making a random 'squiggle' on the drawing paper; the child then adds to this, followed by the therapist and so on in a dialogue until a picture builds up. I also use this method when drawing with some children and it seems that my working with the modelling clay at the same time as Keith led to a similar cooperative creation of images. This is rather like the way in which therapists use thoughts and feeling that arise in themselves (known technically as countertransference) to inform them about what is going on with the client's inner world and their relationship with them which is not expressed in any overt way.

6 The temple at Epidaurus was built in the name of Asklepios and is regarded as an ancient hospital. In a technique that pre-echoes the psychotherapy of today, patients would sleep in chambers below ground and report their dreams to the healer through a small hole in the roof of the chamber. Something else struck me about this. Asklepios was brought up by Chiron (who was half-man and half-horse) who taught him all the healing secrets he knew. It struck me how Keith's models of the two adult male figures in his life (see Figures 11.3 and 11.8) are, like Chiron who was a man only from the waist up, both without torsos. I only note this because it seems to resonate with the theme of Keith's search for healing and healers through many of his images.

7 Becker, E. (1973) *The Denial of Death*. New York: The Free Press/ Macmillan, p. 53. Becker quotes Freud, 'I therefore maintain that the fear of death is to be regarded as an analogue of the fear of castration, and that the situation to which the ego reacts is the state of being forsaken or deserted by the protecting superego – by the powers of destiny – which puts an end to security against every danger'. See Freud, S. (1926) *The Problem of Anxiety*. New York: Norton, pub. 1936, pp. 67ff.

8 Becker, op. cit.
9 During this same session I echoed the sense of containment Keith
   needed and had created for himself with the tramp wrapped in
   his blanket. I found myself making a tube-like container from the
   modelling clay which eventually became shaped into the form of a
   seashell – one of nature's most basic containers for a living creature.
10 *Alive* (1992, dir. Frank Marshall).
11 Just as Keith paired himself in different ways with me, his doctors
    and his mother. Myself and Keith were the Keith-and-therapist pair
    at school, then there was the Keith-and-his-doctor pair at the hospital
    and the pairing of Keith-and-his-mother at home.
12 Becker, op. cit.

INDEX